YOUR ENTREPRENEUR'S JOURNEY

Navigating Confidence and Empowerment For Business Success

by James Connor

TABLE OF CONTENTS

INTRODUCTION 6
CHAPTER 1: DEFINING EMPOWERMENT & CONFIDENCE 8
   Empowerment Concept and Its Implications in Business 8
      Characteristics of an Empowered Individual 9
      Empowered Business Leaders & Their Achievements 11
   The Role of Confidence 14
CHAPTER 2: BUILDING A STRONG FOUNDATION 19
   Self-Awareness 19
      Techniques for Identifying Strengths and Weaknesses 20
         1. SWOT Analysis 20
         2. Feedback From Others 23
         3. Self-Reflection Exercises 26
            3.1. Mindfulness Meditation 26
            3.2. Daily Journaling 26
            3.3. Reflective Reading 27
            3.4. Asking Reflective Questions 27
            3.5. Visualization Exercises 28
         4. Professional Assessments 28
   Setting Clear Goals 30
      Aligning Personal Values with Business Objectives 31
      Crafting Achievable Short-Term and Long-Term Business Goals 33
         SMART Goals 34
         Short-Term Goals 36
         Long-Term Goals 39
   Cultivating Discipline and Consistency 42
      Building Habits for Long-Term Success 42
      Overcoming Procrastination and Maintaining Focus 44
CHAPTER 3: DEVELOPING A GROWTH MINDSET 48
   Reframing Challenges as Opportunities 48
      Tips to Reframe Challenges into Opportunities 49
   Continuous Learning 51
      The Importance of Lifelong Learning in Business 51

  Strategies for Staying Updated with Industry Trends and Skills 54
    1. Subscribe to Industry Publications and Blogs *54*
    2. Engage in Online Learning Platforms *55*
    3. Join Professional Associations and Groups *57*
    4. Engage in Peer Learning *58*
 Adapting to Change 60
  Navigating Uncertainty in Business 60
    1. Develop Contingency Plans *61*
    2. Embrace Agile Methodologies *63*
    3. Foster a Proactive Mindset *65*
  Building Flexibility and Adaptability into Your Career 68

CHAPTER 4: EFFECTIVE COMMUNICATION SKILLS 72
 Active Listening 72
  Techniques for Improving Listening Skills 73
 Articulate Speaking 76
  Communicating Ideas Clearly and Persuasively 76
  Overcoming Public Speaking Fears 79
 Non-Verbal Communication 82
  Observing Facial Expressions 82
  Noticing Gestures 84
  Interpreting Posture 86
  Understanding Eye Contact 88
  Analyzing Tone of Voice 90

CHAPTER 5: NETWORKING & RELATIONSHIP BUILDING 94
 Creating Meaningful Connections 94
  Building a Strong Professional Network 95
  Tips on Building a Strong Professional Network 95
 Leveraging Social Media for Networking 98
 Finding and Engaging Mentors 102
  How to Connect with the Right Mentors 104
 Maintaining Relationships 108

CHAPTER 6: LEADERSHIP AND INFLUENCE 118
 Developing Leadership Qualities 118

Key Traits of Effective Leaders 119
Exercises to Enhance Leadership Skills 120
    1. Vision Board Creation 121
    2. Emotional Intelligence Journaling 124
    3. Decision-Making Simulations 128
    4. Role-Playing Adaptability 132
    6. Integrity Reflection 135

Inspiring and Motivating Others *138*
    1. Lead by Example *138*
        Activity: Model the Way 139
    2. Provide Autonomy and Empowerment *141*
        Activity: Delegate Meaningful Tasks 141
    3. Offer Constructive Feedback *144*
        Activity: Feedback Fridays 144
    4. Foster a Collaborative Environment *147*
        Activity: Team-Building Projects 147
    5. Personalize Your Approach *149*
        Activity: One-on-One Meetings 150

Recognizing and Celebrating Achievements *153*
    1. Public Recognition *153*
        Activity: Recognition Board 154
    2. Personalized Rewards *155*
        Activity: Personalized Appreciation Notes 156
    3. Celebration Events *158*
        Activity: Achievement Celebrations 159
    4. Peer Recognition Programs *161*
        Activity: Peer-to-Peer Recognition 161

Persuasion and Influence *164*
Strategies for Persuading Others in Business 164
    1. Understand Your Audience *164*
    2. Build a Strong Case *166*
    3. Use Emotional Appeals *169*
    4. Establish Common Ground *172*
    5. Address Objections Proactively *174*

CHAPTER 7: LOOKING FORWARD – BUILDING A FUTURE WITH CONFIDENCE 177
Staying Ahead with Technological Advancements 177
Strategies for Integrating New Technologies to Enhance Efficiency and Competitiveness 178
1. Conduct Thorough Research and Assessment 178
2. Develop a Clear Implementation Plan 179
3. Provide Comprehensive Training and Support 180
4. Align Technology with Business Goals 180
Cultivating Sustainable Work-Life Integration 182
Strategies for Cultivating Sustainable Work-Life Integration 182
1. Promote Flexible Work Arrangements 182
2. Set Boundaries 185
3. Encourage Regular Breaks and Vacations 188
CONCLUSION 194

INTRODUCTION

The world is changing, offering new opportunities and challenges rampantly. It's the age when aspiring entrepreneurs and business professionals must have their armory filled with something much more than mere technical skills. The basic foundation of real success in business lies in these underrated qualities: ***empowerment and confidence***. These are not considered good qualities to possess but are mandatory to tread along the unpredictable and competitive journey of modern entrepreneurship.

Empowerment is knowing deep down that, assuredly, you hold the power within your grasp to make decisions and own the journey. This simply means taking one's control, believing in one's capability, and going out of the ordinary into areas to which others could limit one. Where there is empowerment, you are the one steering your destiny: an individual no longer afraid of risks, making bold moves or charting the course in the direction of one's goals with determination and clarity.

On the other hand, confidence is the fuel that keeps you going. Confidence is the inner voice that steadies your mind when you need to fight off doubts, the courage to voice out a unique idea, and the unwavering belief that you can do it. Confidence helps you strive for betterment, stay focused in the face of fallbacks, and remain resilient.

Together, confidence and empowerment make a potent synergy. They allow you to make your dreams immaterial and inspire those who look up to you through real and visionary leadership. But these are not inborn; they are translated into qualities through experience, reflection, and lifelong learning.

Imagine stepping into any room with potential investors, partners, or clients and commanding attention with just your presence. Visualize being confident in yourself and making crucial decisions regarding yourself based on the self-belief founded upon your worth and capability. Now, visualize a professional career whereby challenges are faced not as barriers but as opportunities for progress and innovation. That is facilitation and confidence.

The route to feeling empowered and confident comes with countless self-doubts, social expectations, and a fear of failure for many. There is just too much pressure created by the whole business setup, the market dynamic complexities, and the constant feeling of having to prove oneself. Yet, it is just at these moments of uncertainty that your power and potential are forged.

This book offers you an invitation to a journey of transformation. Congratulations: an urge to be who you indeed are, to cast away all doubt, and to venture into the future characterized by your dreams and by your sweat. Packed with real-life stories of successful entrepreneurs, practical steps, and personal reflections, it will bring you the tools and inspiration you need to build a solid foundation of empowerment and confidence.

You will then learn that empowerment is not of others but by self and others, and it only leads toward providing the supporting atmosphere that allows everyone to flourish when your success turns to serve the greater good. Similarly, confidence is not about arrogance or perfection; it's about having the belief in your ability to learn, grow, and adapt.

The way of every entrepreneur is individual, and with it, the difficulties and victories are also unique. There is no limit to those essentials of empowerment and confidence and the way they work, whether you're trying to get a startup swinging, create growth in a small business, or set new records in the jobs marketplace. They represent the secrets to your success and, by any lasting measure, the realization of your full potential. As you read through this book, you will come to realize that all these aspects of empowerment and confidence are exemplary at your fingertips. They are developed through purposeful practice, taking risks, and dedicating yourself to personal development. You will be inspired to be introspective, to take on hairy, audacious goals, and to build the wherewithal to be relentless in their pursuit.

This book is so much more than business. It is about allowing you to lead a life full of purpose, confidence, and fulfilment. It's what's going to empower you for significant strides, use your strengths, and make you the very best you can be. It is a journey of empowerment and building confidence, and I am excited to walk the journey with you.

CHAPTER 1: DEFINING EMPOWERMENT & CONFIDENCE

> "Empowerment isn't about being given the power to do something; it's about having the confidence and drive to take that power for yourself."
>
> — *Indra Nooyi, Former CEO of PepsiCo*

Indra Nooyi perfectly encapsulates the essence of empowerment and confidence in business. Empowerment doesn't simply come from outside sources; rather, it requires active efforts by individuals to seize opportunities and take charge of their destinies. In this chapter, we investigate how empowerment and confidence manifest themselves within businesses, encouraging individuals to lead, innovate, and excel. By understanding both concepts, we identify traits that distinguish empowered individuals apart and how these qualities can transform both personal and organizational success.

Empowerment Concept and Its Implications in Business

Businesses across all industries have been facing daunting challenges in recent years, highlighted by increasing instances of "brown-out," which refers to employees experiencing disengagement similar to burnout, which leads to dissatisfaction, disengagement, and decreased productivity. Organizations have recognized empowerment's essential role as a strategy against this phenomenon while building a highly motivated and efficient workforce.

Traditional corporate structures tended to take a "top-down" approach, following the directives and vision of upper management. Unfortunately, this approach cannot meet the dynamic demands of today's workforce effectively. Studies published in the Journal of Extension demonstrate that employees empowered through empowerment have higher job satisfaction and organizational commitment levels - giving employees autonomy, resources, and confidence necessary for them to make decisions and take actions that contribute towards organizational success.

Empowerment shifts the emphasis from hierarchical control to collaborative leadership, encouraging employees of all levels to take initiative, innovate, and engage more deeply with their work. Empowerment fosters an atmosphere of trust and respect where employees feel appreciated for their contributions - as a result, empowered workers tend to exhibit higher motivation levels, creativity levels, and resilience levels than their unempowered counterparts.

Characteristics of an Empowered Individual

Empowered individuals exhibit several key characteristics that enable them to thrive in dynamic business environments.

Understanding these traits can help you cultivate them within yourself and your team:

1. Confidence

Confidence is the belief in one's abilities and judgment. As a personal trait, confidence allows individuals to face challenges head-on and approach situations with a sense of assurance and calm. This trait is essential for personal empowerment as it enables individuals to take initiative, make decisions, and pursue their goals with determination.

For example, a confident person might volunteer to lead a new project or speak up during meetings to share their ideas. Their self-assured demeanor helps them navigate uncertainties and maintain focus on their objectives. Confidence, rooted in self-awareness, allows individuals to trust their instincts and capabilities, fostering a proactive and ambitious mindset.

2. Resilience

Resilience is the ability to recover quickly from setbacks and remain focused on long-term goals despite short-term challenges. Research from the Harvard Business Review indicates that resilient individuals are better equipped to handle stress and are more likely to persevere through difficult times, maintaining their productivity and morale.

For instance, an entrepreneur facing a failed business venture might use resilience to analyze what went wrong, learn from the experience, and apply those lessons to their next endeavor. This mindset prevents discouragement and promotes continuous improvement, turning potential failures into valuable learning opportunities.

Resilience is not just about bouncing back from failure; it's about maintaining a positive outlook and a proactive approach in the face of adversity. It involves staying committed to your goals, adapting to new circumstances, and continuously striving for excellence. By building resilience, you can navigate the ups and downs of business with greater ease and confidence, ensuring long-term success.

3. Proactivity

Proactivity is the trait of taking initiative and acting in anticipation of future problems, needs, or changes. It means not waiting for instructions but instead seeking out opportunities to improve and make a difference. According to a study from the Journal of Applied Psychology, proactive individuals are more likely to achieve career success and satisfaction because they actively shape their environment and circumstances.

For example, a proactive employee might identify a potential issue in a project before it escalates, propose a solution, and implement preventative measures. This foresight not only helps in avoiding problems but also demonstrates leadership and commitment to the organization's success.

Proactivity involves being forward-thinking and action-oriented. It requires a willingness to step out of your comfort zone, take calculated risks, and embrace new challenges. By cultivating proactivity, you can drive innovation, enhance your problem-solving skills, and create a positive impact in your workplace.

4. Adaptability

Adaptability is the ability to adjust to new conditions and environments. In the fast-paced and ever-changing business world, being adaptable is crucial for staying relevant and competitive. According to research from the Journal of Organizational Behavior, adaptable individuals are more likely to thrive in dynamic environments and lead successful careers.

An example of adaptability can be seen in employees who quickly learn new technologies and processes, integrating them into their workflow to improve efficiency. Their willingness to embrace change and continuous learning enables them to stay ahead of industry trends and meet evolving business demands.

Adaptability involves being open to new ideas, flexible in your approach, and resilient in the face of change. It requires a growth mindset, where challenges are viewed as opportunities for development rather than threats. By being adaptable, you can navigate uncertainty with confidence and seize new opportunities that drive personal and professional growth.

5. Self-Motivation

Self-motivation is the drive to achieve goals and fulfill personal aspirations without external encouragement. It is a key component of empowerment, as it propels individuals to take initiative and pursue excellence. Research from the Journal of Personality and Social Psychology suggests that self-motivated individuals are more likely to achieve their goals and experience higher levels of job satisfaction.

For instance, a self-motivated entrepreneur might set ambitious targets for their business and work tirelessly to achieve them, even when faced with obstacles. Their inner drive pushes them to keep going, innovate, and improve continuously.

Self-motivation involves setting clear, achievable goals, maintaining a positive attitude, and staying focused on your objectives. It requires discipline, persistence, and a strong sense of purpose. By fostering self-motivation, you can sustain your drive to succeed, overcome challenges, and reach your full potential.

These traits not only contribute to personal success but also inspire and uplift those around you, creating a positive and productive organizational culture.

Empowered Business Leaders & Their Achievements

Because of their commitment to empowerment, many business leaders have achieved remarkable success and left a lasting impact on their industries. These leaders understand that by empowering their teams, they can harness the full potential of their workforce, driving innovation and achieving outstanding results.

The following are some notable examples of empowered business leaders who have made significant strides in their fields:

1. Indra Nooyi

Indra Nooyi, former CEO of PepsiCo, is renowned for her transformative leadership and commitment to employee empowerment. During her tenure, Nooyi emphasized the importance of creating an inclusive and supportive work environment where all employees felt valued and motivated to contribute their best efforts. She introduced initiatives that promoted diversity, work-life balance, and professional development, which significantly boosted employee morale and productivity.

Under Nooyi's leadership, PepsiCo saw substantial growth and innovation. She spearheaded the company's transition towards healthier product offerings and sustainable practices, positioning PepsiCo as a forward-thinking leader in the food and beverage industry. Nooyi's approach to empowerment not only enhanced the company's performance but also cultivated a culture of trust and respect, ensuring long-term success and resilience.

2. Mary Barra

Mary Barra, CEO of General Motors, has made significant strides by prioritizing empowerment within the organization. Barra's leadership focuses on creating a culture of trust and transparency, where employees are encouraged to voice their ideas and take ownership of their work. This approach has been particularly effective in driving innovation and adaptability within GM, enabling the company to navigate the rapidly evolving automotive industry.

Barra's commitment to empowerment is evident in her efforts to promote diversity and inclusion within GM. She has implemented programs aimed at advancing women and minorities in the workplace, ensuring that diverse perspectives are represented at all levels of the organization. This inclusive culture has not only improved employee satisfaction and retention but has also driven creativity and innovation, helping GM maintain its competitive edge in the global market.

3. Satya Nadella

Satya Nadella, CEO of Microsoft, has been instrumental in transforming the company through a culture of empowerment and collaboration. Since taking the helm, Nadella has focused on fostering a growth mindset among employees, encouraging continuous learning and experimentation. His leadership has driven Microsoft to new heights, with a renewed emphasis on cloud computing, artificial intelligence, and digital transformation.

Nadella's approach to empowerment involves breaking down silos within the organization and promoting a more inclusive and collaborative work environment. By valuing diverse perspectives and empowering teams to innovate, Microsoft has been able to adapt to changing market demands and maintain its position as a global technology leader.

4. Jacinda Ardern

Jacinda Ardern, Prime Minister of New Zealand, is celebrated for her empathetic and empowering leadership style. Ardern's approach to governance emphasizes kindness, inclusivity, and collective well-being. During her tenure, she has implemented policies that support social equity, environmental sustainability, and economic resilience, empowering citizens to contribute to a better society.

Ardern's leadership during crises, such as the Christchurch mosque shootings and the COVID-19 pandemic, has been marked by transparency, compassion, and decisive action. Her ability to connect with people and empower them to work together for the common good has made her a respected and influential leader on the global stage.

5. Sundar Pichai

Sundar Pichai, CEO of Alphabet Inc. and its subsidiary Google, is known for his inclusive leadership and commitment to innovation. Pichai's approach to empowerment focuses on creating an environment where employees feel valued and are encouraged to bring their ideas to life. Under his leadership, Google has continued to innovate in areas such as artificial intelligence, cloud computing, and consumer technology.

Pichai has also championed initiatives to increase diversity and inclusion within the tech industry, recognizing the importance of varied perspectives in driving innovation. His leadership style, which combines empathy with strategic vision, has helped Google navigate complex challenges and maintain its status as a leading global technology company.

6. Sheryl Sandberg

Sheryl Sandberg, COO of Meta Platforms, Inc. (formerly Facebook), is a strong advocate for empowerment, particularly for women in the workplace. Sandberg's influential book, "Lean In: Women, Work, and the Will to Lead," encourages women to pursue their ambitions and take on leadership roles. Her initiatives at Meta have focused on creating a more inclusive workplace and supporting employees in balancing their professional and personal lives.

Sandberg's leadership has been instrumental in driving Meta's growth and innovation. She has implemented strategies that empower employees to take ownership of their projects and contribute to the company's success. Her emphasis on mentorship, diversity, and inclusion has inspired many to strive for greater equality and representation in the tech industry.

These leaders illustrate how empowerment can drive exceptional outcomes, both in terms of business achievements and in cultivating a motivated, engaged workforce. By empowering themselves and their teams, they have set new standards for what is possible in business, demonstrating that the path to success is paved with trust, innovation, and resilience.

Understanding and embracing the concept of empowerment is crucial for achieving success in today's business environment. Empowerment fosters a culture of trust, innovation, and resilience, enabling individuals and organizations to thrive. By cultivating the characteristics of empowered individuals and learning from exemplary leaders, you can harness the power of empowerment to drive your own success and contribute meaningfully to your organization.

The Role of Confidence

As discussed previously, confidence is a critical trait of empowered individuals, playing a pivotal role in their ability to lead and innovate effectively. Confidence in the business context goes beyond personal assurance; it directly impacts decision-making, leadership, and overall business performance.

The following are the reasons why confidence is crucial for decision-making, leadership, and overall business performance:

1. Decisive Action

Confident leaders are known for their ability to take swift and decisive actions, especially in critical situations. They trust their judgment and have the courage to take bold steps when necessary. This decisiveness is vital in business, where opportunities and threats can arise unexpectedly, requiring immediate and effective responses. According to Symonds Research, confident leaders are more likely to take calculated risks that can lead to significant innovations and competitive advantages.

When a leader hesitates or second-guess themselves, it can create a ripple effect of uncertainty throughout the organization. Employees look to their leaders for direction, and a confident decision-maker can inspire confidence in their team, leading to more cohesive and concerted efforts toward common goals. This decisive action, backed by confidence, ensures that the organization can move forward swiftly and adaptively, maintaining momentum even in challenging times.

2. Effective Communication

Confidence significantly enhances a leader's ability to communicate effectively. Leaders who are confident in their message can convey their vision and expectations clearly and persuasively. This clarity in communication is essential for aligning the team's efforts and ensuring everyone is on the same page. When employees understand the direction and rationale behind decisions, they are more likely to be engaged and committed to the organizational goals.

Moreover, confident leaders can handle feedback and criticism constructively. They are open to listening to different viewpoints and incorporating them into their decision-making process. This openness not only improves the quality of decisions but also fosters a culture of collaboration and mutual respect. Effective communication driven by confidence helps build stronger relationships within the team, enhancing overall organizational harmony and productivity.

3. Inspiring Trust and Loyalty

Confidence in leadership fosters trust and loyalty among employees. When leaders demonstrate self-assurance, they project reliability and competence, which are critical for building trust. Employees are more likely to feel secure and supported in an environment where leadership is confident and consistent. This trust is a cornerstone of effective teamwork and collaboration.

Trustworthy leaders create a positive organizational culture where employees feel valued and motivated to contribute their best. This loyalty translates to lower turnover rates, higher job satisfaction, and increased productivity. Confident leaders who inspire trust can cultivate a loyal workforce that is committed to the organization's success and willing to go the extra mile to achieve it.

4. Fostering Innovation

Confident leaders are more likely to encourage innovation and creative thinking within their teams. They understand that taking risks is a part of growth and are willing to support their employees in exploring new ideas and approaches. This support empowers employees to think outside the box and develop innovative solutions that can give the organization a competitive edge.

By fostering a safe environment for experimentation, confident leaders reduce the fear of failure that often stifles creativity. Employees are more willing to propose and pursue innovative projects when they know that their leaders have confidence in their abilities and are willing to back them. This culture of innovation leads to continuous improvement and helps the organization stay ahead in the market.

5. Resilience in Adversity

Confidence plays a crucial role in a leader's ability to remain resilient during tough times. Leaders who are confident can maintain their composure and focus under pressure, providing a steadying influence for their teams. This resilience is vital for navigating crises and overcoming setbacks, ensuring that the organization can weather storms and emerge stronger.

Resilient leaders inspire their teams to adopt a similar mindset, fostering a culture of perseverance and adaptability. When employees see their leaders handling adversity with confidence and determination, they are more likely to stay motivated and committed to finding solutions. This collective resilience helps the organization not only survive difficult periods but also thrive in the long run.

While confidence is undeniably beneficial, it is important to distinguish between genuine confidence and overconfidence. Understanding this distinction can help leaders harness the positive aspects of confidence while avoiding the pitfalls associated with overconfidence.

The following outlines the key differences between genuine confidence and overconfidence:

1. Foundation of Self-Awareness vs. Hubris

Genuine confidence is grounded in self-awareness and competence. Confident individuals have a realistic understanding of their strengths and weaknesses. They are aware of their capabilities and continuously seek to improve through learning and experience. This type of confidence is built on a solid foundation of knowledge, skills, and self-reflection.

In contrast, overconfidence stems from hubris—a false sense of superiority. Overconfident individuals tend to overestimate their abilities and underestimate the complexity of tasks or challenges. This inflated self-view can lead to reckless decision-making and a failure to recognize potential risks. Overconfidence is often characterized by a lack of self-awareness and an unwillingness to accept feedback or criticism.

2. Openness to Feedback vs. Dismissiveness

Genuine confidence includes a willingness to listen to others and consider different perspectives. Confident leaders seek out feedback, value diverse opinions, and are open to constructive criticism. This openness allows them to make more informed decisions and foster a collaborative work environment.

Overconfident individuals, however, often dismiss feedback and alternative viewpoints. They may believe that their way is the only correct approach, leading to a rigid and authoritarian leadership style. This dismissiveness can stifle innovation, alienate team members, and result in poor decision-making due to a lack of input from others.

3. Balanced Risk-Taking vs. Recklessness

Confident leaders take calculated risks based on thorough analysis and preparation. They understand the potential consequences of their actions and are prepared to mitigate any downsides. This balanced approach to risk-taking enables them to seize opportunities while protecting their organization from unnecessary harm.

On the other hand, overconfident leaders often engage in reckless behavior. They may take significant risks without adequate consideration or planning, driven by an unfounded belief in their invincibility. This recklessness can lead to catastrophic outcomes, as overconfident individuals are less likely to anticipate and prepare for potential failures.

4. Humility vs. Arrogance

Genuine confidence is accompanied by humility. Confident individuals acknowledge their limitations and give credit to others where it is due. They understand that success is often a collective effort and are willing to share the spotlight with their team members.

Overconfidence, however, is frequently paired with arrogance. Overconfident individuals may believe they are solely responsible for their successes and disregard the contributions of others. This arrogance can damage relationships, reduce team cohesion, and create a toxic work environment.

5. Sustainable Growth vs. Short-Lived Success

Genuine confidence leads to sustainable growth and long-term success. Confident leaders are committed to continuous improvement and are resilient in the face of challenges. Their balanced approach to decision-making and leadership fosters a stable and productive organizational culture.

In contrast, overconfidence often results in short-lived success, if any. The reckless decisions and lack of preparedness characteristic of overconfident individuals can lead to significant setbacks and failures. Over time, the negative consequences of overconfidence can erode trust, damage the organization's reputation, and hinder long-term growth.

While confidence is a vital attribute for successful leadership, it is crucial to differentiate between genuine confidence and overconfidence. Genuine confidence can drive sustainable success, while overconfidence can lead to detrimental outcomes.

In understanding the profound impact of empowerment and confidence, we lay the foundation for personal and organizational success. These principles not only define effective leadership but also create a thriving, innovative, and resilient business environment. With these core attributes established, we can now explore how to build a strong foundation for your entrepreneurial journey in the next chapter.

CHAPTER 2: BUILDING A STRONG FOUNDATION

"Success is not the key to happiness. Happiness is the key to success. If you love what you are doing, you will be successful."

— *Albert Schweitzer, French-German Physician, Theologian, Musician, & Philosopher*

Albert Schweitzer exemplified this concept beautifully through his words. He demonstrated the important relationship between personal satisfaction and professional accomplishment. Achieving success requires understanding oneself deeply and aligning personal values with business objectives; to build such a foundation effectively, this chapter explores self-awareness, setting achievable goals, and fostering discipline and consistency as essential elements in creating sustainable yet fulfilling success paths.

Building a solid foundation requires more than mastery of business strategies and techniques; it means creating an attitude that aligns with your core values, understanding how these translate into your practices, and knowing how they translate. Doing this ensures that every decision, from daily operations to long-term planning, reflects who you truly are while leading to genuine satisfaction and success. Focusing on self-awareness and personal growth equips you with the tools needed to handle challenges with confidence while seizing opportunities with clarity.

In this chapter, we'll look at practical methods to deepen self-awareness, techniques for identifying strengths and weaknesses, the significance of feedback and self-reflection, and how meaningful goals should be set that align with values and aspirations as well as strategies to maintain discipline and consistency - essential ingredients of creating an entrepreneurial journey that's both successful and gratifying.

Self-Awareness

The first thing every aspiring entrepreneur needs to develop is self-awareness. This foundational aspect of personal growth is crucial for understanding your capabilities and limitations. Self-awareness involves a deep and honest evaluation of your strengths and weaknesses, enabling you to leverage your skills effectively while addressing areas that need improvement.

Techniques for Identifying Strengths and Weaknesses

Identifying your strengths and weaknesses is a critical step in building self-awareness.

Here are some effective techniques to help you with this process:

1. SWOT Analysis

A SWOT analysis is a strategic planning tool used to identify and analyze the internal and external factors that can impact the success of a project, business venture, or individual career. The acronym SWOT stands for Strengths, Weaknesses, Opportunities, and Threats.

This analysis provides a comprehensive view of your current situation by categorizing various factors into these four key areas:

1. **Strengths:** Internal attributes and resources that support a successful outcome.
2. **Weaknesses:** Internal attributes and resources that could work against a successful outcome.
3. **Opportunities:** External factors that the entity can capitalize on or use to its advantage.
4. **Threats:** External factors that could cause trouble or pose challenges for the entity.

How you can do it:

Step 1: Gather Information

First, you need to collect relevant information about your business or personal situation. This involves gathering data on your performance, resources, market conditions, and competitive landscape. The goal is to have a detailed and accurate understanding of your current position.

Begin by reviewing internal documents such as financial statements, performance reports, and customer feedback. These documents can provide insights into your strengths and weaknesses. For example, financial statements can reveal areas where your business is performing well and areas where costs might be too high. Customer feedback can highlight what your clients value about your services and what needs improvement.

Additionally, look at external sources of information. This could include market research reports, industry analysis, and news articles about your competitors.

Understanding the broader market trends and the competitive landscape will help you identify opportunities and threats. Collecting this information from a variety of sources ensures that your SWOT analysis is well-rounded and comprehensive.

Involve team members in this process to get diverse perspectives. Different people can provide insights based on their unique experiences and roles within the organization.

Step 2: Identify Strengths

Next, identify your strengths. These are the internal attributes and resources that give you an advantage over others. Think about what you do well, the unique resources you have, and what sets you apart from competitors.

Start by asking questions like:

- *What advantages do we have?*
- *What do we do better than anyone else?*
- *What unique resources can we draw upon that others cannot?*

Your strengths could include a strong brand reputation, a loyal customer base, proprietary technology, or a skilled workforce.

Document these strengths clearly. Be specific and factual. For instance, instead of simply noting ***"good customer service,"*** you could write ***"customer service satisfaction rate of 95% based on recent surveys."*** This specificity helps in understanding the exact nature of your strengths and how they can be leveraged for success.

Step 3: Identify Weaknesses

After strengths, turn your attention to weaknesses. These are the internal factors that could hinder your success. It's crucial to be honest and critical during this step to accurately identify areas for improvement.

Consider questions such as:

- *What areas need improvement?*
- *What resources do we lack?*
- *Where do we get negative feedback from customers?*

Weaknesses could include outdated technology, limited resources, poor location, or skills gaps in your team.

For example, with strengths, be specific about your weaknesses. For example, rather than noting **"poor marketing,"** specify ***"low brand awareness in the target market due to limited marketing budget."*** Clear identification of weaknesses will guide you in developing strategies to address them.

Tip: Regularly review and update your list of weaknesses. As your business evolves, new weaknesses may emerge, and existing ones may be resolved.

Step 4: Identify Opportunities

Opportunities are external factors that you can exploit to your advantage. These could be market trends, economic conditions, or changes in consumer behavior that align with your strengths and capabilities.

To identify opportunities, ask questions like:

- *What market trends can we take advantage of?*
- *Are there changes in regulation that could benefit us?*
- *What needs and desires are not being met by current market offerings?*

Opportunities might include an emerging market segment, technological advancements, or gaps in the competition's offerings.

Document these opportunities clearly and consider how your strengths can help you capitalize on them. For example, if there is a growing demand for eco-friendly products and you have a strong sustainability program, this is a significant opportunity to explore.

Stay informed about industry trends and changes. Regularly reading industry publications and attending relevant conferences can help you stay ahead of opportunities.

Step 5: Identify Threats

Finally, identify threats. These are external factors that could cause trouble for your business. Understanding potential threats allows you to develop strategies to mitigate or avoid them.

Consider questions like:

- *What obstacles do we face?*
- *What are our competitors doing that could impact us?*
- *Are there changes in regulations that could harm us?*

Threats could include economic downturns, increasing competition, changes in consumer preferences, or new regulations.

List these threats and assess their potential impact. For example ***"new environmental regulations may increase production costs by 15%."*** By understanding the severity and likelihood of each threat, you can prioritize which ones to address first.

Develop contingency plans for the most significant threats. Having a plan in place can help you respond quickly and effectively if these threats materialize.

By systematically gathering information and analyzing these factors, you can develop strategies that leverage your strengths, address your weaknesses, capitalize on opportunities, and mitigate threats. This strategic approach is essential for building a strong foundation and achieving long-term success.

2. Feedback From Others

Feedback from others involves seeking insights and observations from colleagues, mentors, peers, and even clients about your performance, behavior, and skills. This external perspective is crucial because it provides a more comprehensive view of your strengths and weaknesses than self-assessment alone. Feedback helps you understand how others perceive your actions and decisions, which can be invaluable for personal and professional growth.

Receiving feedback from others can reveal blind spots that you might not be aware of. It can highlight areas where you excel and areas where you need improvement. This process not only helps you gain a deeper understanding of your abilities but also fosters a culture of openness and continuous improvement within your team or organization.

How you can do it:

Step 1: Identify Key Sources of Feedback

First, identify who you will seek feedback from. This should include a diverse group of individuals who interact with you in different contexts and can provide varied perspectives on your performance. Consider colleagues, managers, subordinates, mentors, peers in your industry, and even clients or customers. Each group can offer unique insights that contribute to a well-rounded understanding of your strengths and weaknesses.

Start by making a list of individuals whose opinions you value and who have a clear understanding of your work and behavior. For example, a mentor can provide guidance on your overall career trajectory, while a colleague might give you specific feedback on your teamwork and communication skills. Clients can offer valuable insights into how well you meet their needs and expectations.

Step 2: Create a Safe and Constructive Environment for Feedback

Once you have identified your sources, it's important to create an environment where they feel comfortable providing honest and constructive feedback. Approach them with an open mind and a willingness to listen without becoming defensive. Make it clear that you value their input and are committed to using their feedback for your personal and professional development.

Initiate the conversation by explaining why you are seeking feedback and how it will help you grow. For example, you might say, ***"I am looking to improve my leadership skills and would appreciate your honest feedback on my performance. Your insights will help me identify areas where I can develop further."*** This approach sets a positive tone and encourages open and honest communication.

Tip: Encourage anonymous feedback if it helps people feel more comfortable sharing their honest opinions. This can be done through online surveys or suggestion boxes.

Step 3: Ask Specific Questions

When seeking feedback, ask specific questions that guide the conversation and ensure you get detailed and actionable insights. General questions like ***"How am I doing?"*** may not yield useful information. Instead, ask targeted questions such as, ***"Can you provide examples of when I demonstrated strong leadership?"*** or ***"What are some areas where you think I could improve my communication skills?"***

Specific questions help the feedback providers focus on particular aspects of your performance and give you clear, actionable advice. This approach also makes it easier for them to recall specific instances and provide detailed feedback.

Step 4: Listen Actively and Reflect

As you receive feedback, listen actively and take notes. Show appreciation for the feedback, regardless of whether it is positive or critical. Avoid interrupting or defending yourself during the feedback session. Instead, focus on understanding the feedback and ask clarifying questions if needed.

After the feedback session:

1. Take time to reflect on the insights you received.
2. Consider how the feedback aligns with your self-assessment and identify any patterns or recurring themes.
3. Reflect on how you can incorporate this feedback into your personal development plan.

Step 5: Act on the Feedback

The final step is to act on the feedback you received. Develop an action plan to address the areas for improvement and leverage your strengths. Set specific, measurable goals based on the feedback and outline the steps you will take to achieve them.

Regularly review your progress and seek follow-up feedback to ensure you are on the right track. This iterative process of seeking feedback, reflecting, and acting on it fosters continuous improvement and helps you achieve your personal and professional goals.

By following these steps, you can effectively gather, reflect on, and act upon feedback to continually improve your performance and achieve success.

3. Self-Reflection Exercises

Self-reflection is a critical component of self-awareness, allowing you to evaluate your actions, thoughts, and experiences to gain deeper insights into your strengths and weaknesses.

Here are several self-reflection exercises to help you enhance your self-awareness:

3.1. Mindfulness Meditation

Mindfulness meditation involves focusing your attention on the present moment observing your thoughts and feelings without judgment. This practice helps you become more aware of your internal experiences and how they influence your behavior.

How to Do It:

1. Find a quiet place where you won't be disturbed.
2. Sit comfortably with your back straight and close your eyes.
3. Take a few deep breaths to relax.
4. Focus on your breath, noticing the sensation of the air entering and leaving your body.
5. When your mind wanders, gently bring your focus back to your breath.
6. Continue this practice for 10-15 minutes each day.

Tip: Start with short sessions and gradually increase the duration as you become more comfortable with the practice.

3.2. Daily Journaling

Journaling involves writing down your thoughts, feelings, and experiences daily. This exercise helps you process your emotions, reflect on your actions, and identify patterns in your behavior.

How to Do It:

1. Set aside 10-15 minutes each day for journaling.
2. Write about your day, focusing on significant events, emotions, and thoughts.
3. Reflect on what went well and what could have been better.
4. Ask yourself questions like, ***"What did I learn today?"*** and ***"How did I handle challenges?"***

5. Review your entries periodically to identify recurring themes and areas for improvement.

Tip: Use prompts to guide your writing if you find it difficult to start. For example, ***"What am I grateful for today?"*** or ***"What challenged me today?"***

3.3. Reflective Reading

Reflective reading involves reading books, articles, or essays that encourage self-reflection and personal growth. As you read, you critically engage with the material, relating it to your own experiences and thoughts.

How to Do It:

1. Choose reading materials that focus on self-improvement, leadership, or personal growth.
2. Take notes while reading, highlighting key points that resonate with you.
3. After reading, reflect on how the material applies to your life.
4. Write a summary of your reflections and any actions you plan to take based on your insights.

Tip: Schedule regular reading time each week to ensure consistency in your reflective reading practice.

3.4. Asking Reflective Questions

Asking yourself reflective questions can help you explore your thoughts and feelings more deeply. These questions should prompt introspection and self-examination.

How to Do It:

1. Set aside time each week for a self-reflection session.
2. Choose a few reflective questions to focus on. Examples include:
   - *"What are my core values, and how do they influence my decisions?"*
   - *"What achievements am I most proud of and why?"*
   - *"What are my biggest challenges, and how can I overcome them?"*
3. Write down your responses and reflect on them.
4. Consider discussing your reflections with a mentor or coach for additional insights.

Tip: Keep a list of reflective questions handy and choose different ones each week to explore various aspects of your life.

3.5. Visualization Exercises

Visualization involves imagining yourself achieving your goals and experiencing success. This exercise helps you clarify your aspirations and identify the steps needed to reach them.

How to Do It:

1. Find a quiet space where you can relax.
2. Close your eyes and take a few deep breaths.
3. Visualize yourself achieving a specific goal. Imagine the details of the situation, including what you are doing, how you feel, and who is with you.
4. Reflect on the steps you took to achieve this goal and any challenges you overcame.
5. Open your eyes and write down your visualization experience and the actions you need to take to make it a reality.

Tip: Practice visualization regularly, especially before important tasks or challenges, to boost your confidence and clarity.

Incorporating these self-reflection exercises into your routine can significantly enhance your self-awareness and personal growth. By regularly engaging in these practices, you can gain valuable insights into your behavior and decision-making, helping you become a more effective and self-aware leader.

4. Professional Assessments

Professional assessments are structured tools designed to evaluate various aspects of your personality, skills, and competencies. These assessments are often based on scientific research and provide detailed, objective feedback that can be difficult to obtain through self-reflection alone. By using these tools, you can gain deeper insights into your strengths and weaknesses, helping you to focus your personal and professional development efforts more effectively.

How you can do it:

Step 1: Choose the Right Assessment

There are many types of professional assessments available, each designed to measure different aspects of your abilities and personality. Common types include personality tests, leadership assessments, and skills evaluations. It's important to choose the assessment that aligns best with your goals and the areas you want to explore.

For example, the Myers-Briggs Type Indicator (MBTI) is a popular personality test that helps you understand your personality type and how it affects your interactions and decision-making. Leadership assessments, such as the Leadership Practices Inventory (LPI), evaluate your leadership behaviors and competencies. Skills evaluations, like those provided by Skillsoft or LinkedIn Learning, measure your proficiency in specific areas such as communication, project management, or technical skills.

Tip: Research different assessments to find the ones that are most relevant to your needs. Consider seeking recommendations from mentors or colleagues who have used these tools.

Step 2: Take the Assessment

Once you have selected the appropriate assessment, the next step is to complete it. Most professional assessments are available online and can be completed at your own pace. Ensure that you are in a quiet environment free from distractions when taking the assessment to provide accurate and thoughtful responses.

Follow the instructions carefully and answer the questions honestly. The accuracy of the assessment results depends on your willingness to provide genuine responses. Avoid overthinking your answers; instead, respond with your initial, instinctive reactions to get the most accurate representation of your traits and abilities.

Step 3: Analyze the Results

After completing the assessment, you will receive a detailed report outlining your results. This report will typically include an analysis of your strengths and weaknesses, along with suggestions for improvement. Review the results thoroughly to understand the key insights about your personality, leadership style, or skills.

Look for patterns and correlations in the data. For example, if multiple aspects of the report highlight a particular strength, it reinforces the importance of leveraging that strength in your professional life. Similarly, if a specific weakness is mentioned repeatedly, it indicates an area that requires focused development.

Step 4: Develop an Action Plan

Based on the insights gained from the assessment, develop an action plan to address your weaknesses and leverage your strengths. Set specific, measurable goals that align with the feedback provided by the assessment. For example, if the assessment highlights a need to improve your communication skills, you might set a goal to take a public speaking course or seek opportunities to present in meetings.

Outline the steps you will take to achieve these goals and set a timeline for reviewing your progress. Regularly revisiting your action plan helps ensure that you stay on track and make meaningful improvements over time.

Tip: Share your action plan with a mentor or coach who can provide guidance and hold you accountable for your progress.

Step 5: Seek Ongoing Feedback

Professional assessments are not a one-time event. To continue growing, seek ongoing feedback from colleagues, mentors, and peers. Use this feedback to adjust your action plan and make continuous improvements. Additionally, consider retaking the assessment periodically to measure your progress and identify new areas for development.

Regularly incorporating feedback into your development process helps you stay aware of your growth and ensures that you are continually working towards your goals.

By choosing the right assessment, carefully analyzing the results, and developing a targeted action plan, you can effectively enhance your personal and professional growth. Regularly seeking feedback and reassessing your progress will help you stay on track and achieve sustained success.

Setting Clear Goals

After developing self-awareness, the next step in building a strong foundation for success is setting clear and achievable goals. Goals provide direction and focus, helping you align your efforts with your aspirations and drive your business forward. This section will cover how to align personal values with business objectives and how to craft achievable short-term and long-term business goals.

Aligning Personal Values with Business Objectives

Your personal values are the fundamental beliefs and principles that guide your behavior and decision-making. These values influence how you perceive success, interact with others, and handle challenges. Aligning your personal values with your business objectives ensures that your work is not only profitable but also fulfilling and meaningful. This alignment can enhance your motivation, commitment, and overall satisfaction with your business endeavors.

How you can do this:

Step 1: Identify Your Core Values

Begin by reflecting on what truly matters to you. Your core values are the guiding principles that influence your decisions and actions. They define your priorities and determine what you consider important in both your personal and professional life.

To identify your core values, start by thinking about past experiences where you felt particularly satisfied or fulfilled. What values were being honored in those moments? Conversely, consider times when you felt unhappy or dissatisfied. What values were being compromised? Reflecting on these experiences can help you pinpoint your most deeply held values.

Additionally, consider the role models or individuals you admire. What values do they embody that resonate with you? This can provide further insight into your own values. You can also review lists of common values and circle those that resonate most with you, then narrow down your list to the top five values that are most important to you.

Step 2: Define Your Business Objectives

Once you have a clear understanding of your core values, the next step is to define your business objectives. Business objectives are specific goals that you aim to achieve through your business activities. These objectives should be aligned with your long-term vision and mission.

Begin by identifying the key areas where you want to make an impact. These could include financial targets, market expansion, product development, customer satisfaction, or social responsibility. Be specific about what you want to achieve in each area. For instance, instead of setting a vague goal like *"increase sales,"* specify *"increase sales by 20% over the next year."*

Ensure that your objectives are realistic and achievable. They should challenge you but also be within your capacity to accomplish. Setting SMART (Specific, Measurable, Achievable, Relevant, Time-bound) goals can help ensure that your objectives are clear and attainable.

Step 3: Align Values with Objectives

With your core values and business objectives clearly defined, the next step is to align them. This alignment ensures that your business activities reflect your personal values, leading to greater fulfillment and satisfaction.

To align your values with your objectives, consider how each objective can be achieved in a way that honors your values. For example, if sustainability is a core value, you might set an objective to reduce your business's carbon footprint by implementing eco-friendly practices. If innovation is important to you, you might focus on developing cutting-edge products or services that push the boundaries of your industry.

Regularly review your business objectives to ensure they remain consistent with your personal values. As your business grows and evolves, you may need to adjust your goals to maintain this alignment. This ongoing process helps ensure that your work continues to be meaningful and aligned with your core beliefs.

Step 4: Communicate Your Values and Objectives

Effectively communicating your values and objectives to your team and stakeholders is crucial for creating a cohesive and motivated organization. When everyone understands and embraces your values, it fosters a sense of shared purpose and commitment.

Start by creating a mission statement that reflects your core values and business objectives. This statement serves as a guiding light for your organization, helping to align everyone's efforts with your vision. Share this mission statement with your team and regularly reinforce it through your actions and decisions.

Encourage open dialogue about values and objectives within your organization. Create opportunities for team members to discuss how their work aligns with the company's mission and how they can contribute to achieving the business objectives. This engagement fosters a culture of transparency and collaboration, enhancing overall motivation and performance.

Step 5: Review and Adjust Regularly

Finally, it's important to regularly review and adjust your alignment of values and objectives. As your business grows and the market evolves, your objectives may need to change. Regularly revisiting your values and objectives ensures that they remain relevant and aligned with your vision.

Set aside time periodically to reflect on your progress and evaluate whether your business activities are still aligned with your personal values. This can involve reviewing your mission statement, assessing your current goals, and gathering feedback from your team and stakeholders.

Make any necessary adjustments to ensure that your values and objectives continue to guide your business effectively. This ongoing process of reflection and adjustment helps maintain alignment and ensures that your work remains fulfilling and purposeful.

Aligning personal values with business objectives is a vital aspect of building a successful and meaningful business. By identifying your core values, defining clear business objectives, and ensuring alignment, you can create a strong foundation for long-term success and fulfillment. Regularly reviewing and communicating your values and objectives fosters a cohesive and motivated organization, driving you closer to achieving your vision.

Crafting Achievable Short-Term and Long-Term Business Goals

With your personal values aligned with your business objectives, the next step is to craft achievable short-term and long-term business goals. Setting clear goals provides a roadmap for your actions and decisions, helping you stay focused and motivated.

SMART Goals

SMART goals are a structured way to set and achieve objectives effectively. The acronym SMART stands for Specific, Measurable, Achievable, Relevant, and Time-bound. This method helps ensure that your goals are clear, realistic, and actionable, providing a solid framework for success.

How you can do it:

Step 1: Make Your Goals Specific

Specific goals clearly define what you want to achieve. Avoid vague statements and focus on precise outcomes. This clarity helps you understand exactly what you need to do and why it's important.

For example, instead of saying ***"improve customer service,"*** you could set a specific goal like ***"reduce customer service response time to under 24 hours."*** This goal precisely states what improvement you are aiming for and sets a clear target to work towards. Specific goals eliminate ambiguity and provide a focused direction for your efforts.

To make your goals specific, ask yourself the following questions:

- *What do I want to accomplish?*
- *Why is this goal important?*
- *Who is involved? Where will it take place?*
- *What resources are required?*

Answering these questions will help you create a detailed and clear goal.

Step 2: Make Your Goals Measurable

Measurable goals allow you to track your progress and determine when you have achieved your objective. This involves defining the criteria or metrics you will use to measure your success.

For example, if your goal is to ***"increase website traffic,"*** you need to specify how you will measure this increase. A measurable goal could be to ***"increase website traffic by 25% over the next six months."*** This goal includes a specific metric (25%) and a timeframe (six months), making it easy to track progress.

To ensure your goals are measurable, determine the key performance indicators (KPIs) you will use. These might include numerical targets, such as percentages, dollar amounts, or other quantifiable measures. Regularly monitor these KPIs to assess your progress and make necessary adjustments to stay on track.

Step 3: Make Your Goals Achievable

Achievable goals are realistic and attainable, given your current resources and constraints. While it's important to set ambitious goals, they should also be within reach to avoid frustration and demotivation.

For example, setting a goal to *"double your sales in one month"* might be unrealistic if you lack the necessary resources or market conditions to support such rapid growth. Instead, a more achievable goal might be *"increase sales by 15% over the next quarter."* This goal challenges you but remains feasible based on your current situation.

To ensure your goals are achievable, consider the resources, time, and support available to you. Assess any potential obstacles and develop strategies to overcome them. Setting incremental goals that build upon each other can also help in achieving larger, long-term objectives.

Step 4: Make Your Goals Relevant

Relevant goals align with your broader business objectives and personal values. They should contribute to your overall mission and help you move closer to your long-term vision.

For example, if your long-term vision is to become a leader in sustainable products, a relevant goal might be to *"launch a new eco-friendly product line by the end of the year."* This goal supports your broader objective of sustainability and aligns with your company's mission.

To ensure your goals are relevant, ask yourself how each goal fits into your larger business strategy. Consider whether achieving this goal will have a meaningful impact on your overall success and whether it aligns with your core values and priorities.

Step 5: Make Your Goals Time-bound

Time-bound goals have a clear deadline or timeframe for completion. This creates a sense of urgency and helps you stay focused on your objectives.

For example, instead of setting a goal to *"improve team collaboration,"* you could set a time-bound goal like ***"implement a new team collaboration tool by the end of the next quarter."*** This goal specifies a clear deadline, motivating you to take action within the given timeframe.

To make your goals time-bound, set specific deadlines for each objective. Consider breaking larger goals into smaller milestones with their own deadlines. This approach helps you manage your time effectively and ensures steady progress toward your goals.

SMART goals provide a structured and effective way to set and achieve your business objectives. By making your goals Specific, Measurable, Achievable, Relevant, and Time-bound, you create a clear roadmap for success. This approach ensures that your efforts are focused, purposeful, and aligned with your overall mission, ultimately leading to greater achievement and fulfillment in your entrepreneurial journey.

Short-Term Goals

Short-term goals are objectives that you aim to achieve within a relatively short period, typically within a year. These goals provide immediate direction and motivation, helping you make incremental progress toward your long-term vision. Setting effective short-term goals involves prioritizing tasks that are manageable and impactful, allowing you to build momentum and demonstrate early successes.

Step 1: Identify Immediate Priorities

Begin by identifying the key areas where you need to focus your efforts in the short term. Consider what aspects of your business require immediate attention to support your long-term objectives. These priorities might include increasing sales, improving customer service, enhancing operational efficiency, or launching a new product.

For example, if your long-term goal is to expand into new markets, a relevant short-term goal might be to conduct comprehensive market research within the next three months.

This goal addresses an immediate need that will provide valuable insights and inform your broader strategy.

To identify immediate priorities, ask yourself questions such as:

- *What are the most pressing issues facing my business right now?*
- *What actions will have the greatest impact on my progress toward long-term goals?*

By focusing on high-priority tasks, you ensure that your short-term efforts are aligned with your overall strategy.

Step 2: Set Specific Targets

Define clear, measurable targets for each priority area. Specific targets provide a clear benchmark for success and help you track your progress. Instead of setting vague goals like ***"improve marketing,"*** specify what improvement looks like, such as ***"increase social media engagement by 20% over the next three months."***

Consider the following example: if enhancing customer satisfaction is a priority, a specific target could be ***"reduce average customer response time to under 24 hours within the next quarter."*** This goal is precise, measurable, and provides a clear timeframe for achievement.

To set specific targets, think about the desired outcome and how you will measure success. Use metrics that are relevant to your business objectives, such as revenue growth, customer satisfaction scores, or productivity rates. Clearly defined targets help you maintain focus and provide a sense of accomplishment as you achieve each milestone.

Step 3: Break Down Goals into Actionable Steps

Breaking down your short-term goals into smaller, actionable steps makes them more manageable and helps you maintain momentum. Each step should be a specific task that contributes to the overall goal, providing a clear path to achievement.

For instance, if your goal is to increase monthly sales by 10% over the next six months, break this goal down into actionable steps such as:

1. Develop and launch a new marketing campaign targeting potential customers.
2. Train the sales team on effective closing techniques.
3. Optimize your website for better conversion rates.
4. Offer limited-time promotions to incentivize purchases.

Each of these steps is a concrete action that moves you closer to your overall goal. By focusing on one step at a time, you can steadily make progress and avoid feeling overwhelmed.

Step 4: Assign Responsibilities and Resources

Ensure that each step of your short-term goals is assigned to specific individuals or teams with the necessary resources to complete the tasks. Clearly defined responsibilities and adequate resources are crucial for successful implementation.

For example, if you plan to develop a new marketing campaign, assign this task to your marketing team and provide them with the budget and tools they need to execute the campaign effectively. Establish clear deadlines and checkpoints to monitor progress and provide support as needed.

By assigning responsibilities and allocating resources, you create accountability and ensure that everyone involved is clear on their role and equipped to succeed.

Step 5: Monitor Progress and Adjust as Needed

Regularly monitoring your progress toward short-term goals is essential for staying on track and making necessary adjustments. Set up regular check-ins to review progress, celebrate successes, and address any challenges that arise.

Use key performance indicators (KPIs) to measure your progress and make data-driven decisions. For example, if your goal is to increase social media engagement, track metrics such as likes, shares, comments, and follower growth. Analyze this data to identify trends and adjust your strategy as needed.

If you encounter obstacles or realize that your initial plan is not yielding the desired results, be flexible and willing to make changes. Adjust your tactics, reallocate resources, or set new targets based on what you learn. This iterative approach ensures continuous improvement and helps you achieve your short-term goals more effectively.

By following these steps, you can create a clear and structured path toward success, building momentum and laying the groundwork for achieving your long-term business objectives.

Long-Term Goals

With your short-term goals providing immediate direction and momentum, it's equally important to set long-term goals that guide your overall business strategy and vision. Long-term goals typically span several years and require strategic planning and sustained effort. These goals help you chart a course for your business's future, ensuring that your day-to-day actions align with your broader aspirations.

Step 1: Define Your Vision

Begin by defining your long-term vision for your business. Think about where you want your business to be in the next three to five years. Consider aspects such as growth targets, market expansion, product development, and your company's impact on the industry.

For instance, if your vision is to become a leader in sustainable products, your long-term goals might include developing a comprehensive line of eco-friendly products and achieving a significant market share in the green industry. This vision provides a clear and inspiring direction for your business.

To define your vision, reflect on your core values, mission, and the unique strengths of your business. Consider the impact you want to make and the legacy you wish to create. A compelling vision serves as a motivational force, guiding your strategic decisions and actions.

Step 2: Set Strategic Objectives

Once you have a clear vision, translate it into specific, strategic objectives. These objectives should be ambitious yet attainable, providing a roadmap for achieving your long-term vision. Strategic objectives are broader and more encompassing than short-term goals, requiring detailed planning and resource allocation.

For example, if your vision is to expand into international markets, a strategic objective could be to *"establish a presence in three new countries within the next five years."* This objective outlines a clear target and timeframe, providing a foundation for detailed planning.

To set effective strategic objectives, consider the following:

- **Market Analysis:** Conduct thorough market research to identify opportunities for expansion and growth. Understand the competitive landscape and customer needs in potential new markets.
- **Resource Assessment:** Evaluate the resources required to achieve your objectives, including financial investments, human capital, and technological capabilities.
- **Risk Management:** Identify potential risks and develop strategies to mitigate them. This proactive approach helps ensure that your objectives are realistic and achievable.

Step 3: Develop a Detailed Roadmap

Creating a detailed roadmap is essential for turning your strategic objectives into actionable plans. This roadmap outlines the steps needed to achieve your long-term goals, breaking them down into manageable phases and milestones.

For instance, if your objective is to launch a new product line, your roadmap might include the following phases:

1. **Research and Development:** Conduct market research, develop prototypes, and test product concepts.
2. **Production Planning:** Establish production processes, source materials, and set up manufacturing facilities.
3. **Marketing Strategy:** Develop a comprehensive marketing plan, including branding, advertising, and distribution channels.
4. **Launch and Scale:** Launch the product, monitor initial performance and scale production based on demand.

Each phase should have specific milestones and deadlines, ensuring steady progress toward your long-term goal. Regularly reviewing and updating your roadmap helps you stay on track and adapt to changing circumstances.

Step 4: Allocate Resources and Responsibilities

Achieving long-term goals requires careful resource allocation and a clear delegation of responsibilities. Ensure that you have the necessary financial, human, and technological resources to support your strategic objectives.

For example, if expanding into new markets is a priority, you might need to invest in market research, hire local experts, and establish partnerships with distributors. Assign specific tasks to team members or departments, providing them with the resources and support needed to succeed.

To allocate resources effectively, consider the following:

- **Budget Planning:** Develop a detailed budget that outlines the financial investments required for each phase of your roadmap. Monitor expenses regularly to ensure you stay within budget.
- **Talent Management:** Identify the skills and expertise needed to achieve your objectives. Hire, train, and develop your team to ensure they can meet the demands of your long-term goals.
- **Technology and Tools:** Invest in the technology and tools necessary to support your strategic initiatives. This might include software, equipment, or infrastructure upgrades.

Step 5: Monitor Progress and Adjust as Needed

Regularly monitoring your progress toward long-term goals is crucial for ensuring that you stay on track and can make necessary adjustments. Set up regular check-ins to review progress, celebrate achievements, and address any challenges that arise.

Use key performance indicators (KPIs) to measure your success and make data-driven decisions. For instance, if your goal is to expand into new markets, track metrics such as market share growth, revenue from new markets, and customer acquisition rates.

If you encounter obstacles or realize that your initial plan is not yielding the desired results, be flexible and willing to make changes. Adjust your tactics, reallocate resources, or revise your objectives based on what you learn. This iterative approach ensures continuous improvement and helps you achieve your long-term goals more effectively.

By following these steps, you can create a structured and motivated path toward success, ensuring that your efforts are focused, purposeful, and aligned with your overall mission. This approach not only drives sustained growth but also helps you achieve fulfillment and satisfaction in your entrepreneurial journey.

Cultivating Discipline and Consistency

Being disciplined and consistent is crucial for achieving long-term success in business. These qualities help you stay focused on your goals, maintain productivity, and overcome obstacles. By building effective habits and developing strategies to combat procrastination, you can cultivate the discipline and consistency needed to sustain growth and achieve your objectives.

Building Habits for Long-Term Success

Building positive habits is essential for maintaining discipline and achieving long-term success. Habits are the routines and behaviors that you perform regularly, often without conscious thought. When these habits are aligned with your goals, they can significantly enhance your productivity and effectiveness.

Here are several tips to help you cultivate effective habits that will sustain your growth and achievement over time:

1. Start Small

One of the most effective strategies for building lasting habits is to start small. By beginning with manageable tasks, you reduce the likelihood of feeling overwhelmed and increase the chances of sticking with the new behavior. For example, if you aim to incorporate regular exercise into your routine, start with just five minutes a day rather than committing to an hour-long session. This incremental approach makes the habit easier to adopt and maintain.

As the small habit becomes ingrained, its complexity and duration gradually increase. This gradual buildup helps reinforce the behavior without causing burnout. Over time, what started as a simple, manageable task can evolve into a significant, beneficial habit that supports your long-term goals.

2. Create a Consistent Routine

Consistency is key to forming lasting habits. Establishing a daily routine helps reinforce your habits and ensures they become an integral part of your day. Design a routine that aligns with your peak productivity times and includes the habits you want to develop.

For example, if you are most productive in the morning, schedule important tasks and habit-building activities during this time.

A well-structured routine provides a framework that guides your actions, making it easier to prioritize essential tasks and maintain focus. Consistency in your routine not only strengthens your habits but also enhances overall productivity and efficiency. Ensure that your routine is realistic and flexible enough to accommodate unexpected changes or challenges.

3. Use Triggers and Rewards

Triggers and rewards are powerful tools for reinforcing habits. A trigger is a cue that initiates the habit, while a reward provides positive reinforcement, making it more likely that you will repeat the behavior. Identify triggers that can prompt your desired habits. For instance, if you want to develop a habit of reading daily, you could use your morning coffee as a trigger to start reading.

Pair the habit with a reward to reinforce the behavior. For example, after completing a reading session, you might reward yourself with a short break or a favorite snack. The anticipation of the reward can motivate you to stick with the habit, while the consistent association between the trigger and the habit helps solidify the routine.

4. Stay Accountable

Accountability is a crucial factor in maintaining discipline and building lasting habits. Share your goals and habits with a friend, mentor, or accountability partner who can provide support and encouragement. Regular check-ins with your accountability partner can help you stay on track and address any challenges you encounter.

Being part of a supportive community or group with similar goals can also provide additional motivation and accountability. When you know that others are aware of your commitments and progress, you are more likely to stay disciplined and adhere to your habits. This external support system can be instrumental in overcoming obstacles and maintaining long-term consistency.

5. Track Your Progress

Monitoring your progress is essential for building and maintaining habits. Keeping a habit tracker allows you to visualize your progress and stay motivated. Each time you complete a habit, mark it on your tracker. Seeing a streak of successful days can provide a sense of accomplishment and encourage you to continue.

A habit tracker can also help you identify patterns and areas where you might need to make adjustments. For example, if you notice that you consistently miss certain habits on specific days, you can analyze the reasons and make changes to your routine or environment to support better adherence. Regularly reviewing your progress helps you stay focused and committed to your long-term goals.

6. Be Patient and Kind to Yourself

Building habits takes time and effort, and it's important to be patient and kind to yourself throughout the process. There will be days when you might slip up or face challenges that disrupt your routine. Instead of being overly critical, acknowledge these setbacks as a natural part of the journey and refocus on your goals.

Practice self-compassion by treating yourself with the same kindness and understanding you would offer to a friend. Recognize that forming new habits is a gradual process, and it's normal to encounter difficulties along the way. Celebrate your progress, no matter how small, and remind yourself that each step forward is a positive move toward achieving your long-term success.

By integrating these tips into your daily life, you can develop and sustain positive habits that support your goals and drive your business toward sustained growth and achievement.

Overcoming Procrastination and Maintaining Focus

Procrastination is a common barrier to productivity and success. Overcoming procrastination and maintaining focus requires a combination of strategies that address both the mental and practical aspects of this challenge.

Here are several tips to help you stay on track and achieve your goals:

1. Identify and Address Procrastination Triggers

Understanding what triggers your procrastination is the first step in overcoming it. Common triggers include fear of failure, perfectionism, lack of motivation, and feeling overwhelmed. By identifying these triggers, you can develop strategies to manage and mitigate them.

To identify your triggers:

1. Reflect on situations where you tend to procrastinate and consider the underlying reasons. For example, if you delay starting projects, it might be due to a fear of failure or perfectionism.
2. Keep a journal to document instances of procrastination and analyze patterns. Note the specific tasks you procrastinate on and the thoughts or feelings that accompany them.
3. Once you identify your triggers, develop strategies to address them. For instance, if fear of failure is a trigger, practice self-compassion and focus on the learning process rather than the outcome.

Breaking tasks into smaller, more manageable steps can help reduce feelings of overwhelm and make it easier to start.

2. Create a Productive Work Environment

A well-organized and distraction-free work environment is essential for maintaining focus and overcoming procrastination. Your physical space can significantly impact your ability to concentrate and be productive.

To create a productive work environment:

1. Declutter your workspace and remove any unnecessary items that could distract you. Keep only the essentials on your desk.
2. Optimize your environment for comfort and efficiency. Ensure proper lighting, a comfortable chair, and an ergonomic setup.
3. Minimize digital distractions by turning off non-essential notifications and using tools that block distracting websites or apps during work periods.

Establish a dedicated workspace separate from areas associated with relaxation or leisure. This physical separation helps create a mental boundary between work and rest.

3. Use Time Management Techniques

Effective time management is crucial for overcoming procrastination and maintaining focus. By organizing your time efficiently, you can ensure that tasks are completed promptly and avoid last-minute rushes.

To manage your time effectively:

1. Use techniques like the Pomodoro Technique, which involves working in short, focused intervals (typically 25 minutes) followed by a short break. This method helps maintain concentration and prevent burnout.
2. Plan your day with a to-do list or schedule, prioritizing tasks based on their importance and deadlines. Allocate specific time blocks for each task and stick to the schedule.
3. Set aside time for regular breaks to rest and recharge. Breaks help prevent fatigue and maintain productivity throughout the day.

Tip: At the end of each workday, review your progress and plan for the next day. This practice helps you start each day with a clear sense of purpose and direction.

4. Practice Self-Compassion and Positive Self-Talk

Negative self-talk and harsh self-criticism can contribute to procrastination by increasing feelings of anxiety and inadequacy. Practicing self-compassion and positive self-talk can help you maintain a positive mindset and stay motivated.

To practice self-compassion and positive self-talk:

1. Acknowledge your feelings without judgment. Understand that procrastination is a common challenge and that it's okay to struggle with it occasionally.
2. Replace negative thoughts with positive affirmations. For example, instead of thinking, ***"I'll never get this done,"*** remind yourself, ***"I have the skills and resources to complete this task."***
3. Focus on your progress rather than perfection. Celebrate small achievements and use them as motivation to continue moving forward.

Tip: Develop a daily affirmation routine to reinforce positive self-talk. Write down a few encouraging statements and repeat them to yourself each morning.

5. Find an Accountability Partner

Having an accountability partner can provide the support and motivation needed to overcome procrastination and stay focused. An accountability partner is someone who checks in on your progress and helps keep you on track.

To find and work with an accountability partner:

1. Choose someone who is reliable and has similar goals or interests. This could be a friend, colleague, or mentor.
2. Set regular check-ins to discuss your goals, progress, and challenges. Use these meetings to provide mutual support and encouragement.
3. Be honest about your struggles and achievements. Accountability works best when both parties are open and committed to helping each other succeed.

Tip: Consider joining a study group, mastermind group, or online community focused on productivity and goal achievement. These groups provide a broader network of support and accountability.

By implementing these strategies, you can enhance your productivity, stay on track with your goals, and achieve long-term success in your entrepreneurial journey.

By embracing self-awareness, setting clear goals, and cultivating discipline and consistency, you lay a robust foundation for your business endeavors. These principles not only guide your daily actions but also ensure long-term success and fulfillment. As you continue to build upon this foundation, you will be well-equipped to navigate the complexities of entrepreneurship and achieve your vision.

CHAPTER 3: DEVELOPING A GROWTH MINDSET

"Your time is limited, so don't waste it living someone else's life. Don't be trapped by dogma – which is living with the results of other people's thinking. Don't let the noise of others' opinions drown out your own inner voice. And most important, have the courage to follow your heart and intuition."

– Steve Jobs, Former CEO of Apple

Steve Jobs' words emphasize the significance of taking steps toward self-realization and innovation, with courage. Embark on an entrepreneurial journey while viewing challenges as opportunities, adapting quickly to changes, and continuously learning from experience. This chapter explores these principles, which will turn obstacles into stepping stones that pave your journey to sustained business success.

An adaptable and resilient mindset aren't interchangeable: cultivating one involves seeing potential where others see problems and understanding that every setback offers an opportunity to learn and grow. A growth mindset can make the difference in any business context where being agile enough to pivot or innovate quickly can determine success or failure; by adopting this perspective, you're positioning yourself not just to endure challenges but to thrive from them!

This chapter offers practical strategies for cultivating a growth mindset, showing you how reframing challenges, committing to lifelong learning, and accepting adaptability can lead to personal and professional excellence. Experienced practitioners provide actionable tips that show how leveraging this power will enable you to navigate business world uncertainty more successfully while reaching long-term goals more swiftly.

Reframing Challenges as Opportunities

Challenges are inevitable in business, but how you perceive and respond to them can make all the difference. Embracing challenges with a positive outlook transforms them into opportunities for growth and innovation. This mindset shift helps you stay motivated and resilient, even when faced with significant obstacles.

Reframing challenges involves changing your perspective from seeing difficulties as threats to viewing them as chances to learn and grow. This proactive approach encourages creative problem-solving and continuous improvement. By developing this mindset, you can turn setbacks into stepping stones for success.

Tips to Reframe Challenges into Opportunities
1. Focus on Learning and Growth

Every challenge presents a learning opportunity. When you encounter a problem, focus on what you can learn from the experience rather than the difficulty itself. This perspective helps you gain valuable insights and develop new skills.

Sara Blakely, the founder of Spanx, faced numerous rejections when she first started pitching her product. Instead of getting discouraged, she used each rejection as a learning experience to refine her pitch and improve her product. Her persistence and willingness to learn from failure eventually led to the success of Spanx, making her one of the youngest self-made female billionaires.

You can adopt this approach by asking yourself questions like:

- *What can I learn from this situation?*
- *How can this challenge help me grow?*

By focusing on the lessons rather than the setbacks, you cultivate a mindset geared towards continuous improvement and resilience.

2. Embrace Change and Adaptability

Change often brings challenges, but it also offers opportunities for innovation and growth. Embracing change means being open to new ideas and approaches and willing to adapt to shifting circumstances.

Howard Schultz, the former CEO of Starbucks, embraced change when he transformed the small coffee bean retailer into a global coffeehouse chain. Facing initial resistance and numerous operational challenges, Schultz's ability to adapt and innovate led to the creation of a unique customer experience that revolutionized the coffee industry.

To emulate this, be proactive in seeking out new opportunities that come with change. Stay flexible and open-minded, and consider how changes in the market or industry trends can be leveraged to your advantage. Regularly reviewing your business strategy and being willing to pivot when necessary can help you stay ahead of the curve.

3. Practice Resilience and Persistence

Resilience and persistence are key to overcoming challenges. Resilience helps you bounce back from setbacks, while persistence keeps you moving forward despite difficulties.

Thomas Edison, one of the greatest inventors, exemplified resilience and persistence. He famously failed thousands of times before successfully inventing the electric light bulb. Instead of seeing his failures as setbacks, Edison viewed them as steps toward success, famously stating, ***"I have not failed. I've just found 10,000 ways that won't work."***

You can build resilience by maintaining a positive outlook and developing coping strategies for stress and setbacks. Persistence can be fostered by setting clear goals, maintaining focus, and celebrating small victories along the way. Remember that each failure is a step closer to success and an opportunity to refine your approach.

4. Seek Support and Collaboration

Challenges can be more manageable when you seek support and collaborate with others. Leveraging the strengths and insights of a team can lead to innovative solutions and shared success.

Elon Musk, CEO of Tesla and SpaceX, often highlights the importance of collaboration in overcoming challenges. Faced with numerous technical and financial obstacles, Musk has consistently relied on his teams' expertise and collaborative efforts to achieve groundbreaking advancements in electric vehicles and space exploration.

To apply this tip, build a strong support network of mentors, colleagues, and industry peers. Don't hesitate to ask for help or advice when facing a challenge. Collaborative brainstorming and problem-solving can lead to creative solutions that you might not have discovered on your own.

5. Reframe Negative Thoughts

Changing the way you think about challenges can significantly impact your ability to handle them. Reframe negative thoughts into positive or neutral ones to maintain a constructive mindset.

For example, instead of thinking, ***"This problem is too difficult to solve,"*** reframe it to, ***"This is a challenging problem, but it's an opportunity to develop a new skill or find a better solution."*** This shift in thinking can reduce stress and increase your motivation to tackle the issue.

Reframing negative thoughts involves mindfulness and self-awareness. Pay attention to your inner dialogue and consciously replace negative statements with positive affirmations. Over time, this practice can help you develop a more optimistic and proactive approach to challenges.

By adopting these strategies, you can transform obstacles into valuable experiences that drive your personal and professional growth.

Continuous Learning

With the fast-paced and ever-evolving nature of today's business environment, continuous learning is more critical than ever. Committing to lifelong learning ensures that you remain competitive, adaptable, and innovative in your field. This section will explore the importance of lifelong learning in business and provide strategies for staying updated with industry trends and skills.

The Importance of Lifelong Learning in Business

Lifelong learning is the ongoing, voluntary, and self-motivated pursuit of knowledge for personal or professional development.

In the context of business, it is essential for several reasons:

1. Adaptability and Competitiveness

In today's fast-paced business environment, staying adaptable and competitive is crucial. Lifelong learning helps you keep up with technological advancements, market shifts, and evolving consumer preferences. By continuously updating your skills and knowledge, you can adapt to changes more quickly and effectively.

For example, as new technologies emerge, businesses that adopt and integrate these innovations can gain a significant competitive edge. Lifelong learning enables you to stay ahead of industry trends and capitalize on new opportunities. Companies that encourage continuous learning among their employees are better positioned to innovate and respond to market demands.

Furthermore, lifelong learning fosters a culture of continuous improvement within organizations. Employees who are committed to learning are more likely to seek out new ways to enhance their performance and contribute to the company's success. This proactive approach to personal and professional development helps maintain a competitive edge in an ever-changing business landscape.

2. Personal and Professional Growth

Engaging in lifelong learning fosters both personal and professional growth. It enhances cognitive abilities, boosts confidence, and expands your skill set. This growth leads to greater job satisfaction and opens up new career advancement opportunities.

Lifelong learning allows you to pursue new interests and develop expertise in areas that complement your career goals. For instance, taking courses in leadership, project management, or digital marketing can make you more versatile and valuable to your organization. This continuous development not only benefits your current role but also prepares you for future challenges and responsibilities.

Moreover, lifelong learning promotes a growth mindset—a belief that abilities and intelligence can be developed through dedication and hard work. This mindset encourages you to embrace challenges, persist in the face of setbacks, and view effort as a path to mastery. As a result, you become more resilient and better equipped to navigate the complexities of the business world.

3. Innovation and Creativity

Continuous learning encourages curiosity and creativity, essential components of innovation. Exposure to new ideas, perspectives, and knowledge can inspire innovative thinking and problem-solving.

For example, learning about different industries or disciplines can spark creative solutions that you can apply to your business. Cross-disciplinary knowledge allows you to draw connections between seemingly unrelated fields, leading to breakthrough innovations. Organizations that foster a culture of lifelong learning are more likely to encourage experimentation and creative thinking among their employees.

Additionally, staying informed about the latest trends and advancements keeps you at the forefront of innovation. Whether it's adopting new technologies, exploring emerging markets, or developing innovative products and services, continuous learning provides the insights and skills needed to drive business growth and differentiation.

4. Enhanced Leadership and Decision-Making

Lifelong learning is particularly important for leaders. Effective leadership requires staying informed about industry trends, understanding new management practices, and continuously developing one's skills. Leaders who commit to lifelong learning are better equipped to make informed decisions and guide their organizations through change.

By staying updated with the latest research and best practices, leaders can implement strategies that enhance organizational performance. For instance, learning about new leadership models or team dynamics can improve how leaders motivate and manage their teams. This ongoing development ensures that leaders remain relevant and capable of addressing the complex challenges facing their organizations.

Moreover, lifelong learning helps leaders cultivate a culture of learning within their organizations. When leaders prioritize their own development, they set a positive example for their teams, encouraging employees to pursue their professional growth. This culture of learning fosters a dynamic and agile organization that can thrive in a rapidly changing business environment.

5. Better Problem-Solving and Critical Thinking

Continuous learning sharpens your problem-solving and critical-thinking skills. These skills are crucial for identifying and addressing business challenges effectively. By engaging in diverse learning experiences, you can develop a broader perspective and more sophisticated analytical abilities.

For example, studying case studies, attending workshops, and participating in discussions can enhance your ability to evaluate complex situations and make sound decisions. These activities expose you to different viewpoints and problem-solving techniques, helping you approach challenges with greater creativity and confidence.

Additionally, lifelong learning encourages reflective thinking—a practice of analyzing past experiences to gain insights and improve future performance. Reflective thinking helps you learn from successes and failures, refining your approach to problem-solving and decision-making over time.

By committing to continuous learning, you can stay ahead of industry trends, adapt to changing circumstances, and achieve sustained success in your entrepreneurial journey.

Strategies for Staying Updated with Industry Trends and Skills

Staying current with industry trends and skills requires a proactive approach to learning and professional development.

Here are several strategies to help you stay updated:

1. Subscribe to Industry Publications and Blogs

Subscribing to industry publications and blogs involves regularly reading content from reputable sources that focus on your specific industry. These sources provide in-depth analyses, expert opinions, and updates on the latest trends, innovations, and challenges. By keeping up with these publications, you can stay informed about the latest developments and gain valuable insights that can help you make better business decisions.

How you can do this:

Step 1: Identify Reputable Sources

Start by identifying reputable publications and blogs that are relevant to your industry. Look for sources that are well-regarded by industry experts and peers. Some popular examples include industry-specific magazines, trade journals, professional association publications, and influential blogs written by thought leaders.

It is important to select sources that provide accurate and unbiased information. To do this, ask colleagues and mentors for recommendations or search for top-rated industry publications online. Websites like Feedly or Flipboard can help you aggregate content from multiple sources into a single feed, making it easier to stay organized and up-to-date.

Step 2: Set Up Subscriptions and Notifications

Once you have identified the relevant sources, subscribe to their newsletters, RSS feeds, or social media channels to receive regular updates. Most industry publications and blogs offer free or paid subscriptions that deliver the latest articles directly to your inbox. Setting up notifications ensures that you don't miss important updates and can read new content as soon as it is published.

For blogs, consider using a feed reader like Feedly, which allows you to compile and categorize multiple blog feeds in one place. This makes it easier to manage your reading list and ensures that you have quick access to the latest posts.

Step 3: Dedicate Regular Time for Reading

To make the most of your subscriptions, dedicate regular time to reading and reflecting on the content. Integrate this practice into your daily or weekly routine. For example, you might set aside 30 minutes each morning to read through industry news or reserve time at the end of the week to catch up on the most insightful articles.

Taking notes on key points and actionable insights can help you retain the information and apply it to your business. Keeping a journal or digital document of your reflections can be a useful reference for future decision-making.

Tip: Create a reading schedule that fits your routine and stick to it. Consistency is key to staying informed and leveraging the knowledge you gain.

By subscribing to industry publications and blogs, you stay informed about the latest trends, innovations, and challenges in your field. This proactive approach to learning keeps you competitive and equipped to make informed decisions, ensuring your business remains at the forefront of the industry.

2. Engage in Online Learning Platforms

Online learning platforms, such as Coursera, LinkedIn Learning, and Udemy, provide access to a vast array of courses covering various topics. These courses are typically designed and taught by industry professionals and academic experts, ensuring high-quality content. Online learning allows you to learn at your own pace, making it easier to fit education into your busy schedule.

How to Do It

Step 1: Identify Relevant Courses

Begin by identifying the skills and knowledge areas you want to develop. Reflect on your career goals, industry demands, and any gaps in your current expertise. Use the search and filter functions on online learning platforms to find courses that match your needs.

For example, if you want to improve your digital marketing skills, you might look for courses on SEO, social media marketing, or content strategy. Read course descriptions, reviews, and ratings to ensure the course content is relevant and of high quality.

Step 2: Enroll and Schedule Learning Time

Once you've identified the relevant courses, enroll in them. Many platforms offer both free and paid courses, with the latter often providing more comprehensive content and certification upon completion. Make sure to review the course syllabus and requirements to understand what is expected.

To stay consistent, create a learning schedule that fits into your daily or weekly routine. Dedicate specific times for studying, just as you would for any other important task. Setting regular study sessions helps build a habit and ensures steady progress.

Step 3: Engage Actively with the Content

Actively engaging with the course material is crucial for effective learning. Take notes, participate in discussion forums, and complete all assignments and quizzes. Engaging with the content helps reinforce learning and allows you to apply new knowledge practically.

Many platforms offer interactive elements such as video lectures, hands-on projects, peer reviews, and live sessions. Utilize these resources to enhance your understanding and retention of the material. Participating in discussions with other learners can also provide different perspectives and deepen your insights.

Engaging in online learning platforms offers a flexible and effective way to stay current with industry trends and develop new skills.

3. Join Professional Associations and Groups

Professional associations and groups are organizations that bring together individuals from the same profession or industry. These associations offer various benefits, including access to exclusive industry reports, training programs, certifications, webinars, workshops, and conferences. They also provide a platform for networking with peers, industry leaders, and potential mentors.

How to Do It

Step 1: Identify Relevant Associations

Start by identifying professional associations and groups that are relevant to your industry. Look for organizations that are well-regarded and have a strong reputation in your field. These might include national or international associations, as well as local chapters or special interest groups.

To find relevant associations, ask colleagues and mentors for recommendations, conduct online research, and review industry publications that list top professional organizations.

Examples include:

- The American Marketing Association (AMA) for marketing professionals.
- The Project Management Institute (PMI) for project managers.
- The Society for Human Resource Management (SHRM) for HR professionals.

Step 2: Become a Member

Once you have identified the relevant associations, join as a member to gain access to their resources and benefits. Membership often requires an annual fee, which provides access to exclusive content, discounted rates for events and training programs, and opportunities to connect with industry professionals.

Visit the association's website to learn about membership tiers and benefits. Some associations offer student or early-career memberships at reduced rates. Complete the membership application process and start exploring the resources available to you.

Step 3: Participate Actively

Active participation is key to maximizing the benefits of professional associations. Attend webinars, workshops, and conferences to stay informed about the latest trends and best practices. These events often feature expert speakers and panel discussions that provide valuable insights.

Engage with other members through forums, discussion groups, and networking events. Share your experiences, ask questions, and contribute to discussions. Building relationships with peers and industry leaders can lead to mentorship opportunities, collaborations, and career advancement.

Joining professional associations and groups provides ongoing support and opportunities for continuous learning and networking. By actively participating in these organizations, you can stay informed about industry trends, enhance your professional development, and build a strong network of peers and mentors. This proactive approach helps you stay competitive and advance your career in a rapidly changing business environment.

4. Engage in Peer Learning

Peer learning involves learning from and with others in a collaborative setting. This can take place through various formats, such as study groups, knowledge-sharing sessions, collaborative projects, or informal discussions. By sharing insights, experiences, and best practices, peers can help each other understand complex topics, solve problems, and stay informed about industry developments.

How to Do It

Step 1: Organize Knowledge-Sharing Sessions

Start by organizing regular knowledge-sharing sessions with your colleagues or peers. These sessions can be formal or informal and can cover a wide range of topics relevant to your industry. The goal is to create a platform where everyone can contribute their knowledge and learn from each other.

To organize a knowledge-sharing session:

1. Identify common interests or areas where team members want to improve.
2. Set a regular schedule for these sessions, such as weekly or monthly meetings.
3. Assign a facilitator for each session to guide the discussion and ensure everyone has an opportunity to contribute.

During these sessions, encourage participants to share their experiences, discuss recent industry trends, and present case studies or new findings. This collaborative approach fosters a culture of continuous learning and mutual support.

Step 2: Participate in Collaborative Projects

Engage in collaborative projects with your peers to learn from their expertise and experiences. Working together on projects allows you to apply new knowledge and skills in a practical context, enhancing your learning experience.

To participate in collaborative projects:

1. Identify projects that require diverse skill sets and knowledge.
2. Form teams with members who have complementary skills and experiences.
3. Establish clear goals, roles, and responsibilities for each team member.

Collaborative projects provide hands-on learning opportunities and help you develop teamwork, communication, and problem-solving skills. Additionally, working closely with peers can lead to innovative solutions and new perspectives on challenges.

Step 3: Encourage Open Communication

Promote a culture of open communication and knowledge sharing within your organization. Encourage team members to share their insights, experiences, and best practices, both formally and informally.

To encourage open communication:

- Create channels for knowledge sharing, such as dedicated Slack channels, internal forums, or regular team meetings.

- Recognize and reward contributions to knowledge sharing to motivate team members to participate.
- Foster an environment where everyone feels comfortable sharing their ideas and asking questions.

Open communication helps break down silos and ensures that valuable knowledge and insights are accessible to everyone in the organization. This collaborative environment enhances collective learning and drives continuous improvement.

Tip: Create a structured format for peer learning sessions to ensure they are productive and focused on relevant topics. This might include setting agendas, preparing discussion points, and summarizing key takeaways.

Engaging in peer learning provides valuable insights and collaborative experiences, helping you stay updated with industry trends and continuously develop your skills. This approach not only enhances individual learning but also strengthens the overall capabilities of your team or organization.

By implementing these strategies, you can ensure continuous learning and professional development, positioning yourself and your business for long-term success.

Adapting to Change

Change is a constant in the business world, and the ability to adapt to it is crucial for long-term success. Whether it's shifts in market trends, technological advancements, or unexpected crises, navigating change effectively can mean the difference between thriving and struggling. This section will explore strategies for navigating uncertainty in business and building flexibility and adaptability into your career.

Navigating Uncertainty in Business

Navigating uncertainty in business involves preparing for the unknown and being able to respond swiftly to unexpected events. This requires a proactive mindset, strategic planning, and effective leadership.

The following are key strategies for navigating uncertainty in business:

1. Develop Contingency Plans

Contingency planning involves creating backup plans for various scenarios that could impact your business. This preparedness allows you to respond quickly and effectively when faced with unexpected challenges.

For example, during the COVID-19 pandemic, businesses that had contingency plans for remote work were able to transition more smoothly compared to those that did not. Companies like Dropbox and Twitter, which already had flexible work policies and technology in place, could quickly adapt to the new remote working environment, ensuring business continuity and minimizing disruptions.

How to Create Contingency Plans:

Step 1: Identify Key Risks

Identifying key risks is the first step in contingency planning. Use the results of your SWOT analysis to pinpoint potential threats to your business. These risks could include natural disasters, economic downturns, supply chain disruptions, or cyber-attacks.

To do this:

1. Gather your team and brainstorm possible scenarios that could negatively impact your operations.
2. Consider both internal and external factors.
3. Once you have a list of potential risks, prioritize them based on their likelihood and potential impact. This will help you focus on the most critical threats that require immediate attention.

Identifying key risks allows you to understand where your business is most vulnerable and lays the foundation for developing effective contingency plans.

Step 2: Develop Scenarios

For each identified risk, develop detailed scenarios outlining the potential impact on your business operations. Consider best-case, worst-case, and most likely outcomes for each scenario. This helps you understand the range of possible effects and prepares you for different levels of disruption.

To create these scenarios, begin by analyzing how each risk could unfold. For example, if you identified a supply chain disruption as a key risk, consider how a minor delay, a significant slowdown, or a complete halt in supplies would affect your operations. Detail the specific consequences of each level of disruption, such as delays in product delivery, increased costs, or loss of customer trust.

Next, key stakeholders should be involved in these discussions to gain diverse perspectives and insights. This collaborative approach ensures that you cover various angles and implications of each scenario. Document these scenarios thoroughly, outlining the potential chain of events and their impacts on different areas of your business.

Developing scenarios helps you visualize potential challenges and prepare for various outcomes, ensuring that your business is better equipped to handle disruptions.

Step 3: Create Action Plans

Once you have developed scenarios for each key risk, create specific action plans to address them. These plans should include clear steps and responsibilities, ensuring that your team knows what to do in each situation.

To create action plans, start by defining the immediate actions that need to be taken when a risk materializes. For instance, if a cyber-attack occurs, your action plan might include steps such as isolating affected systems, notifying stakeholders, and implementing data recovery procedures. Assign specific roles and responsibilities to team members to ensure a coordinated response.

Additionally, communication protocols should be established to keep everyone informed during a crisis. This includes setting up a chain of command, identifying key contacts, and outlining the methods for internal and external communication.

Creating detailed action plans ensures that your team can respond quickly and effectively to minimize the impact of any disruption.

Step 4: Test and Review Plans

Regularly testing and reviewing your contingency plans is crucial to ensure their effectiveness. Conduct drills or simulations to practice your response to different scenarios and identify any weaknesses or gaps in your plans.

To test your plans, simulate a variety of scenarios and evaluate how well your team responds. For example, you might conduct a mock cyber-attack to test your IT security measures and response procedures. After each drill, debrief with your team to discuss what worked well and what needs improvement.

Review and update your contingency plans periodically to keep them current. This involves incorporating feedback from drills, addressing any changes in your business environment, and ensuring that all contact information and resources are up to date.

Testing and reviewing your plans helps you refine your strategies and ensures that your team is well-prepared to handle real-life disruptions.

2. Embrace Agile Methodologies

Agile methodologies involve iterative planning, continuous feedback, and adaptive processes. These practices focus on delivering small, incremental changes rather than large, infrequent updates. This approach allows teams to respond quickly to new information, customer feedback, and changing market conditions. Agile emphasizes collaboration, transparency, and a willingness to adapt, making it well-suited for navigating uncertainty and driving innovation.

How to Do It

Step 1: Form Cross-Functional Teams

Creating cross-functional teams is a cornerstone of agile methodologies. These teams are composed of members from different departments who bring diverse skills and perspectives to the table. This diversity enhances problem-solving and innovation, as team members can collaborate closely and learn from each other.

To form cross-functional teams:

- Identify key projects or initiatives that would benefit from a collaborative approach.
- Select team members from various departments, such as marketing, sales, IT, and operations.
- Ensure that each team has the necessary skills and resources to achieve its goals.
- Cross-functional teams foster a culture of collaboration and shared responsibility, driving more effective and innovative solutions.

Step 2: Adopt Iterative Planning

Iterative planning involves breaking down projects into smaller, manageable tasks that can be completed in short development cycles, often called sprints. Each sprint typically lasts two to four weeks and culminates in a review where the team assesses progress and plans the next cycle.

To adopt iterative planning:

1. Define the overall project goal and break it into smaller, achievable milestones.
2. Plan the tasks for the first sprint, ensuring they are specific, measurable, and achievable within the sprint duration.
3. Conduct daily stand-up meetings to track progress, identify obstacles, and make necessary adjustments.

At the end of each sprint, hold a review meeting to evaluate the outcomes, gather feedback, and plan the next sprint. This iterative approach enables continuous improvement and allows teams to respond quickly to changes.

Step 3: Implement Continuous Feedback

Continuous feedback is essential for agile methodologies. Regularly gathering feedback from stakeholders, customers, and team members ensures that the project stays aligned with expectations and can be adjusted as needed.

To implement continuous feedback:

1. Schedule regular feedback sessions with stakeholders and customers to review progress and gather input.
2. Use tools like surveys, user testing, and focus groups to collect feedback on specific aspects of the project.
3. Encourage team members to provide feedback during sprint reviews and daily stand-ups.

Actively incorporating feedback helps teams stay aligned with user needs and market demands, enhancing the relevance and quality of their work.

Step 4: Promote a Culture of Adaptability

A culture of adaptability is crucial for agile methodologies to thrive. Encourage a mindset where change is seen as an opportunity rather than a threat and where continuous learning and improvement are valued.

To promote adaptability:

- Encourage Experimentation: Allow teams to try new approaches and learn from their successes and failures.
- Provide Training: Offer workshops and resources on agile principles and practices to help team members develop their skills.

Creating an adaptable culture empowers teams to respond swiftly to changing conditions and fosters a proactive approach to problem-solving.

Tip: Use agile project management tools like Jira or Trello to facilitate collaboration, track progress, and manage tasks effectively.

By embracing agile methodologies, you can enhance your business's ability to adapt to change, drive innovation, and continuously improve. This approach not only helps you navigate uncertainty but also positions your business for long-term success in a dynamic environment.

3. Foster a Proactive Mindset

Being proactive means anticipating potential challenges and opportunities before they arise, allowing you to stay ahead of the curve and respond effectively to changes. Cultivating a proactive mindset is essential for business leaders and teams aiming to thrive in uncertain environments.

Here are several tips to help you foster a proactive mindset within your organization:

1. Encourage Forward-Thinking

Encourage forward-thinking by regularly discussing future trends, potential disruptions, and emerging opportunities. This helps shift the focus from reactive problem-solving to proactive planning.

For example, conduct quarterly strategy sessions where you analyze industry reports, market forecasts, and technological advancements. Engage team members in brainstorming sessions to explore how these trends might impact your business and what steps you can take to prepare.

Encouraging forward-thinking not only helps you stay prepared but also fosters a culture of innovation and continuous improvement.

2. Invest in Continuous Learning

Continuous learning is a key component of a proactive mindset. By staying informed about the latest developments in your industry, you can anticipate changes and adapt more quickly.

Promote a learning culture by providing access to online courses, industry conferences, and professional development programs. Encourage employees to pursue certifications and attend workshops that enhance their skills and knowledge.

Regularly sharing insights and learnings from these experiences during team meetings can help disseminate knowledge throughout the organization and inspire others to engage in continuous learning.

3. Emphasize Scenario Planning

Scenario planning involves imagining various future scenarios and developing strategies to address them. This approach helps you prepare for a range of possibilities and enhances your ability to respond effectively to unforeseen events.

To implement scenario planning, create a dedicated team to explore different "what if" scenarios. These scenarios should cover a spectrum of potential events, from economic shifts to technological breakthroughs and regulatory changes. Develop detailed action plans for each scenario, outlining the steps your business would take to mitigate risks and capitalize on opportunities.

Emphasizing scenario planning helps ensure that your organization is well-prepared for multiple future outcomes, reducing uncertainty and increasing resilience.

4. Promote Open Communication

Open communication is vital for fostering a proactive mindset. Encouraging transparent and frequent communication ensures that everyone in the organization is aware of potential challenges and opportunities.

Create platforms for regular updates and discussions, such as all-hands meetings, internal newsletters, and collaborative tools like Slack or Microsoft Teams. Encourage team members to share their insights, concerns, and suggestions openly.

When communication flows freely, it becomes easier to identify emerging issues early and develop proactive solutions collaboratively.

5. Recognize and Reward Proactivity

Recognizing and rewarding proactive behavior reinforces its importance and encourages others to adopt a similar approach. Acknowledge team members who take initiative, suggest innovative ideas, or anticipate and solve problems before they escalate.

Implement recognition programs that highlight and reward proactive efforts. This could include formal awards, public acknowledgment in team meetings, or opportunities for career advancement.

By celebrating proactive behavior, you create a positive feedback loop that motivates the entire organization to embrace a forward-thinking attitude.

6. Develop a Risk Management Culture

A proactive mindset involves being prepared for risks and having strategies in place to manage them. Developing a risk management culture helps your team anticipate and mitigate potential threats.

Encourage risk assessment as part of your regular business processes. Train employees on identifying and evaluating risks and involve them in developing risk mitigation strategies. Use tools like risk matrices to prioritize risks based on their likelihood and impact.

Regularly review and update your risk management plans to ensure they remain relevant and effective. By embedding risk management into your organizational culture, you enhance your ability to anticipate and address potential challenges proactively.

Tip: Encourage a mindset where every team member feels responsible for identifying and addressing risks, fostering a sense of collective ownership and vigilance.

By adopting these practices, you can better anticipate and respond to changes, ensuring your business remains resilient and competitive in a dynamic environment. This proactive approach not only prepares you for the future but also drives innovation and long-term success.

Navigating uncertainty in business requires a proactive mindset, agile methodologies, and effective contingency planning. By adopting these strategies, you can enhance your organization's resilience and adaptability, ensuring you remain competitive and capable of thriving amidst change.

Building Flexibility and Adaptability into Your Career

Flexibility and adaptability are key traits that allow professionals to navigate their careers successfully, even when faced with unexpected changes or disruptions. Flexibility means being willing to modify your plans and embrace new opportunities. Adaptability involves the capacity to learn quickly, adjust your strategies, and remain resilient in the face of challenges.

Building these traits into your career requires a proactive approach to learning, personal development, and mindset cultivation.

Here are some tips for building flexibility and adaptability into your career:

1. Embrace Diverse Experiences

Engaging in a variety of roles and projects can significantly enhance your flexibility and adaptability. Diverse experiences expose you to different challenges, work environments, and problem-solving approaches, which can broaden your skill set and perspective.

To do this, seek out opportunities that push you beyond your comfort zone. This might include taking on new projects that require different skills, working with teams from different departments, or even exploring opportunities in different industries. For instance, volunteering for a cross-departmental task force can give you insights into other parts of the business and help you develop new competencies.

Additionally, consider lateral moves within your organization. These moves can provide valuable experiences that enhance your understanding of the business and prepare you for higher-level roles. Embracing diverse experiences helps you become more versatile and capable of adapting to various career scenarios.

2. Develop a Growth Mindset

A growth mindset is the belief that abilities and intelligence can be developed through effort and learning. Cultivating a growth mindset helps you embrace challenges and view setbacks as opportunities for growth.

To develop a growth mindset:

- Focus on continuous learning and self-improvement.
- Seek feedback from peers and mentors to identify areas for development.

Rather than viewing mistakes as failures, see them as valuable learning experiences that contribute to your professional growth.

Practicing resilience in the face of challenges is also crucial. This involves maintaining a positive attitude and perseverance even when things don't go as planned. By fostering a growth mindset, you'll be more inclined to take on new challenges and adapt to changing circumstances.

3. Stay Technologically Savvy

Keeping up with technological advancements is essential for adaptability in today's rapidly evolving work environment. Staying technologically savvy ensures that you can leverage new tools and platforms to enhance your productivity and remain competitive.

To stay updated, regularly participate in training programs and workshops focused on new technologies relevant to your field. Follow tech news and trends, subscribe to industry publications, and join online forums discussing technological innovations.

Implementing new technologies in your work processes can also demonstrate your adaptability to employers and colleagues. For example, mastering new project management software or utilizing data analytics tools can significantly enhance your efficiency and effectiveness.

4. Foster Emotional Intelligence

Emotional intelligence (EI) is the ability to recognize, understand, and manage your own emotions and those of others. High EI contributes to better interpersonal relationships, effective communication, and conflict resolution—all of which are critical for flexibility and adaptability.

To foster emotional intelligence, practice self-awareness by reflecting on your emotional responses and their impact on your behavior. Develop empathy by actively listening to others and considering their perspectives. Enhance your social skills by engaging in open and constructive communication, and practice self-regulation by managing stress and maintaining composure under pressure.

By improving your emotional intelligence, you can navigate social complexities in the workplace more effectively, build stronger relationships, and adapt to various interpersonal dynamics.

These traits enable you to navigate the complexities of a dynamic career landscape, ensuring long-term success and resilience in the face of change. By proactively cultivating these skills, you position yourself to thrive in any professional environment.

Adapting to change is essential for long-term success in an ever-evolving business landscape. By building flexibility and adaptability into your career, you equip yourself with the skills and mindset needed to thrive amidst uncertainty and seize new opportunities. Embrace change as a catalyst for growth and innovation, ensuring your continued progress and resilience.

By developing a growth mindset, embracing continuous learning, and adapting to change, you lay a solid foundation for navigating the complexities of the business world. These principles not only help you overcome obstacles but also empower you to seize opportunities and drive sustained success. As you continue to build on this foundation, you'll be well-prepared to face whatever challenges come your way and thrive in your entrepreneurial journey.

CHAPTER 4: EFFECTIVE COMMUNICATION SKILLS

"Communication is the most important skill any leader can possess."

– Richard Branson, English Business Magnate

Richard Branson's words illuminate the essential role communication plays in leadership and business success. Skillful communication skills form the foundation of relationships, clearly communicating ideas and managing complex interactions. In this chapter we'll cover essential components of effective communication such as active listening, articulate speaking and nonverbal interactions; mastering these abilities can substantially enhance professional interactions and outcomes.

Effective communication in business can set you apart as both a leader and collaborator. Not just what but how and when we say things matter greatly when creating positive working environments. Communication involves more than simply speaking aloud - it requires understanding others, clearly expressing thoughts, adapting messages to differing audiences, adapting messages for different contexts or audiences, and adapting responses appropriately. Communication skills are integral for reaching goals while simultaneously cultivating an enjoyable work environment.

This chapter offers practical strategies and techniques for honing your communication skills. From mastering active listening techniques to conquering public speaking fears, you'll discover ways to interact more effectively with others, build stronger relationships, increase influence, and boost leadership abilities. By the time this chapter concludes, you will possess the confidence and tools necessary for communicating clearly and impactfully ensuring your message resonates and drives action.

Active Listening

Active listening is a communication technique that involves fully concentrating, understanding, responding, and remembering what is being said. Unlike passive listening, where you might hear the words but not truly engage with the speaker, active listening requires intentional effort to understand the speaker's message and respond thoughtfully. This skill is crucial in building strong relationships, enhancing collaboration, and fostering a productive work environment.

The following is how active listening significantly impacts building and strengthening relationships in various contexts, particularly in the workplace:

1. **Fostering Trust and Respect:** Active listening fosters trust and respect between individuals. When you actively listen, you show that you value the speaker's thoughts and feelings. This demonstration of respect can build mutual trust, which is essential for any strong relationship. Trust and respect are the bedrock of effective teamwork, leading to a more harmonious and cooperative work environment.
2. **Enhancing Collaboration and Teamwork:** Effective collaboration relies on clear and open communication. Active listening ensures that team members fully understand each other's ideas, needs, and concerns, which is crucial for collaborative efforts. When team members feel heard, they are more likely to contribute their best work and support their colleagues.
3. **Reducing Misunderstandings and Conflicts:** Misunderstandings often arise from poor communication. Active listening helps to clarify messages and ensure that everyone is on the same page. By reflecting on and summarizing what has been said, you can confirm your understanding and address any ambiguities immediately.
4. **Building Emotional Connections:** Active listening helps build emotional connections by showing empathy and understanding. When people feel emotionally connected, they are more likely to engage in positive interactions and support each other. This is especially important in leadership roles, where understanding and addressing the emotional needs of team members can significantly impact their motivation and performance.
5. **Improving Employee Morale and Engagement:** When employees feel that their voices are heard and their opinions matter, they are more likely to be engaged and motivated. Active listening can boost employee morale by making them feel valued and appreciated. This increased engagement can lead to higher productivity, job satisfaction, and retention rates.

Active listening is a powerful tool for building and strengthening relationships in the workplace. By honing your active listening skills, you can create a more supportive and effective work environment, leading to better outcomes for both individuals and the organization as a whole.

Techniques for Improving Listening Skills
Improving your active listening skills requires deliberate practice and a commitment to truly understanding and engaging with the speaker.

Here are several techniques to help you become a more effective listener:

1. Maintain Eye Contact

Maintaining eye contact is crucial for active listening as it shows the speaker that you are fully engaged and interested in what they are saying. Eye contact helps build a connection and encourages the speaker to continue sharing.

How to Do It:

1. Focus on the speaker's eyes without staring intensely. Aim for a natural, comfortable level of eye contact.
2. Occasionally nod or smile to show you are following the conversation.
3. Avoid distractions such as checking your phone or looking around the room.

Consistent eye contact demonstrates your attentiveness and helps foster a deeper connection with the speaker.

2. Avoid Interrupting

Interrupting the speaker can disrupt their train of thought and signal that you are not fully engaged. Allowing them to finish their thoughts shows respect and ensures you have the complete context before responding.

How to Do It:

1. Let the speaker finish their sentences and ideas without interjecting.
2. If you have a question or comment, make a mental note and wait for an appropriate pause in the conversation.
3. Practice patience and focus on fully understanding the speaker's message before responding.

By avoiding interruptions, you show that you value the speaker's perspective and are committed to understanding their message.

3. Provide Feedback

Providing feedback through verbal and non-verbal cues reassures the speaker that you are actively listening. It also helps you stay engaged and better retain the information being shared.

How to Do It:

1. Use verbal affirmations such as *"I see," "I understand,"* or *"That makes sense"* to indicate you are following along.
2. Nod your head or smile to show agreement or understanding.
3. Mirror the speaker's emotions subtly to demonstrate empathy and connection.

Offering feedback through these small gestures encourages the speaker and enhances the flow of the conversation.

4. Summarize and Reflect

Summarizing and reflecting on what the speaker has said confirms your understanding and helps clarify any potential misunderstandings. This technique also reinforces your comprehension and retention of the information.

How to Do It:

1. Paraphrase the speaker's main points using phrases like, *"So, what you're saying is..."* or *"If I understand correctly, you feel that..."*.
2. Reflect on the emotions or concerns expressed by the speaker. For example, *"It sounds like you're feeling frustrated about..."*.
3. Ask follow-up questions to delve deeper into the topic and ensure you have captured the full message.

Summarizing and reflecting not only show that you are listening but also help solidify your understanding and build rapport with the speaker.

5. Ask Open-Ended Questions

Asking open-ended questions encourages the speaker to elaborate on their points and provides more insight into their thoughts and feelings. This technique promotes a richer and more meaningful conversation.

How to Do It:

1. Use questions that require more than a yes or no answer, such as *"Can you tell me more about that?"* or *"What are your thoughts on...?"*.
2. Follow up on specific points the speaker has made to encourage further discussion.
3. Be genuinely curious and interested in the speaker's perspective, allowing the conversation to flow naturally.

By asking open-ended questions, you demonstrate your interest and commitment to understanding the speaker's message, fostering a deeper and more engaging dialogue.

By incorporating these techniques into your daily interactions, you can become a more effective listener, build stronger relationships, and create a more collaborative and productive work environment.

Articulate Speaking

Speaking articulately involves expressing your ideas clearly and persuasively. It is a critical skill for effective communication in business, helping you convey your thoughts in a way that others can easily understand and respond to. Mastering this skill can enhance your ability to lead, influence, and collaborate with others.

Communicating Ideas Clearly and Persuasively

Having the ability to communicate ideas clearly and persuasively is essential in the business world. It enables you to convey your thoughts effectively, influence others, and achieve your goals.

The following techniques will help you communicate your ideas more clearly and persuasively:

1. Be Concise and Direct

Clarity and conciseness are crucial for effective communication. Being concise means delivering your message in as few words as necessary without losing the essence of what you want to convey. This approach prevents misunderstandings and keeps your audience engaged.

How to Do It:

Step 1: Organize Your Thoughts

Before you start speaking, take a moment to organize your thoughts. Identify the key points you want to convey and arrange them logically. This helps you stay on track and avoid unnecessary digressions. For instance, you might outline your main message, supporting details, and conclusion. This structure ensures that your communication is coherent and easy to follow.

Step 2: Use Simple Language

Avoid jargon and complex language that might confuse your audience. Instead, use straightforward, everyday language that is easy to understand. For example, instead of saying ***"We need to leverage synergies to optimize our operational efficiencies,"*** you could say ***"We need to work together to improve our operations."*** Simple language ensures that your message is accessible to everyone, regardless of their background.

Step 3: Get to the Point

State your main message early in the conversation to capture your audience's attention. Begin with a clear and direct statement of your main point, followed by the necessary details. For example, if you are proposing a new project, start with ***"I propose we launch a new marketing campaign to increase our brand visibility,"*** and then provide the supporting details. This approach ensures that your audience understands the purpose of your communication right from the start.

By being concise and direct, you ensure that your message is clear and easily understood, making it more effective and memorable.

2. Structure Your Message

A well-structured message enhances comprehension and retention. Structuring your message involves organizing your content logically and clearly.

How to Do It:

Step 1: Start with an Introduction

Begin with a brief introduction that outlines the main topic and what you aim to achieve. This sets the stage for your audience and provides context for your message. For instance, you might say, ***"Today, I'd like to discuss our new project plan and its expected benefits."***

Step 2: Present the Main Points

Clearly present each main point, providing relevant details and examples to support them. Use transitional phrases to guide your audience from one point to the next. For example, ***"Firstly, we need to focus on market research. Secondly, we should develop a strong marketing strategy. Lastly, we need to monitor*** *our progress regularly."* This logical flow helps your audience follow your argument more easily.

Step 3: Conclude Effectively

Summarize the key points and conclude with a clear call to action or closing thought. For example, ***"In conclusion, by implementing these strategies, we can significantly boost our market presence. I recommend we start the project next month and allocate the necessary resources."*** This reinforces your message and provides a clear direction for your audience.

A structured message helps your audience follow along and understand your ideas more easily, making your communication more effective.

3. Engage with Your Audience

Engaging with your audience makes your communication more interactive and impactful. Active engagement helps maintain interest and encourages participation.

How to Do It:

Step 1: Make Eye Contact

Maintain eye contact to create a connection with your audience and show that you are focused on them. This helps build rapport and keeps the audience engaged. For example, during a presentation, make sure to look at different members of the audience rather than staring at your notes or slides.

Step 2: Use Gestures and Expressions

Incorporate natural gestures and facial expressions to emphasize your points and convey enthusiasm. This makes your communication more dynamic and helps convey your message more effectively. For instance, using hand movements to illustrate points or smiling to show positivity can enhance your delivery.

Step 3: Encourage Interaction

Ask questions, invite feedback, and encourage discussion to involve your audience in the conversation. This makes the interaction more engaging and helps you gauge your audience's understanding and reactions. For example, ***"What do you think about*** *this approach?"* or *"Do you have any questions or suggestions?"* Encouraging interaction fosters a two-way dialogue and makes your audience feel valued.

Engaging with your audience makes your communication more dynamic and memorable, fostering a stronger connection and better understanding.

These skills enhance your ability to influence and lead effectively, ensuring your messages are understood and impactful.

Overcoming Public Speaking Fears

Public speaking can be intimidating, but overcoming this fear is essential for effective communication. Building confidence in public speaking involves preparation, practice, and positive mindset techniques.

Here is how you can do it:

Step 1: Prepare Thoroughly

Thorough preparation is the foundation of confident public speaking. Knowing your material well reduces anxiety and increases your confidence. Ensure you have a deep understanding of your topic. Gather all necessary information and organize it logically. This helps you feel more in control and knowledgeable, which can significantly reduce anxiety.

You can start by creating an outline of your speech or presentation, breaking it down into an introduction, main points, and conclusion. This structure ensures that your content flows logically and is easy to follow. Practice your speech multiple times, both alone and in front of a practice audience, to become familiar with the content and delivery.

In addition to mastering your material, anticipate potential questions and prepare answers. This not only boosts your confidence but also ensures you are ready to handle any inquiries from your audience. The more prepared you are, the more at ease you will feel when it's time to speak.

Step 2: Practice Regularly

Practice is crucial for building confidence and reducing public speaking anxiety. The more you practice, the more comfortable you become with your material and delivery style.

Start by practicing in front of a mirror to observe your body language and facial expressions. Pay attention to your posture, gestures, and eye contact. This self-awareness helps you refine your non-verbal communication and project confidence.

Next, practice in front of a small, supportive audience, such as friends, family, or colleagues. Ask for constructive feedback to identify areas for improvement. Gradually increase the size of your practice audience to simulate the experience of speaking to a larger group. This incremental approach helps you build confidence and adjust to different audience sizes.

Step 3: Visualize Success

Visualization is a powerful technique that can help reduce anxiety and boost confidence. By imagining yourself speaking confidently and successfully, you create a positive mental image that can influence your actual performance.

Take a few moments each day to close your eyes and visualize yourself delivering your speech. Picture the setting, the audience, and your own demeanor. Imagine yourself speaking clearly, engaging with the audience, and receiving positive feedback. This mental rehearsal helps create a sense of familiarity and confidence.

Incorporate positive affirmations into your visualization practice. Repeat statements like "I am a confident and effective speaker" or "I am well-prepared and capable." These affirmations reinforce a positive mindset and reduce self-doubt.

Step 4: Focus on Your Message, Not Yourself

Shifting your focus from your fear to the importance of your message can help reduce anxiety. When you concentrate on delivering valuable information to your audience, you are less likely to be preoccupied with your own nervousness.

Remind yourself why your message matters and how it can benefit your audience. This shift in perspective helps you prioritize the value of your content over your fear of public speaking. Engage with your audience by making eye contact and encouraging interaction, which can help you feel more connected and less self-conscious.

Concentrate on the content of your speech and how best to communicate it. Use storytelling, examples, and anecdotes to make your message relatable and engaging. By focusing on your message, you can deliver a more compelling and confident presentation.

Step 5: Manage Physical Symptoms

Public speaking anxiety often manifests as physical symptoms such as sweating, trembling, or a rapid heartbeat. Managing these symptoms can help you maintain composure and confidence during your speech.

Practice deep breathing exercises to calm your nerves and reduce physical tension. Inhale deeply through your nose, hold for a few seconds, and exhale slowly through your mouth. This technique helps slow your heart rate and promotes relaxation.

Incorporate physical activities such as stretching or light exercise before your speech to release nervous energy and improve blood flow. Staying hydrated and avoiding caffeine can also help manage physical symptoms of anxiety.

Step 6: Seek Constructive Feedback and Reflect

After each public speaking opportunity, seek constructive feedback to identify areas for improvement and build on your strengths. Constructive criticism helps you grow as a speaker and enhances your confidence over time.

Ask trusted colleagues, mentors, or audience members for their feedback on your delivery, content, and overall performance. Reflect on their suggestions and consider how you can implement them in future speeches.

Keep a journal of your public speaking experiences, noting what went well and what you can improve. This reflection helps you track your progress, celebrate your successes, and learn from each experience.

Articulate speaking involves communicating ideas clearly and persuasively and overcoming public speaking fears. By mastering these skills, you can enhance your ability to lead, influence, and collaborate effectively, ensuring your messages are understood and impactful.

Non-Verbal Communication

Being able to read and interpret non-verbal cues is equally important as using them effectively. This skill allows you to understand the unspoken messages and emotions of others, improving your ability to respond appropriately and build stronger relationships.

Observing Facial Expressions

Facial expressions are powerful non-verbal cues that can convey a wide range of emotions and reactions. They include movements of the facial muscles, such as smiles, frowns, raised eyebrows, and furrowed brows. These expressions can provide insights into a person's feelings, intentions, and responses, often more accurately than their words.

How You Can Do It

Step 1: Learn the Basic Emotions

Start by familiarizing yourself with the basic emotions that are universally expressed through facial expressions. These include happiness, sadness, anger, surprise, fear, and disgust. Recognizing these expressions will help you identify the underlying emotions in your interactions.

- **Happiness:** Look for raised cheeks, crow's feet wrinkles around the eyes, and an upturned mouth (smile).
- **Sadness:** Notice drooping eyelids, a downturned mouth, and a slight frown.
- **Anger:** Identify furrowed brows, tight lips, and flared nostrils.
- **Surprise:** Look for raised eyebrows, wide-open eyes, and a dropped jaw.
- **Fear:** Observe wide-open eyes, raised upper eyelids, and a slightly open mouth.
- **Disgust:** Look for a wrinkled nose, raised upper lip, and narrowed eyes.

Step 2: Observe Contextual Cues

While basic facial expressions are universal, the context in which they occur is crucial for accurate interpretation. Pay attention to the situation, the person's words, and their overall body language to understand the context of their facial expressions.

For example, a smile during a happy announcement is likely genuine, while a smile during a tense negotiation might be a polite social gesture rather than a true expression of happiness. Considering the context helps you differentiate between genuine and social expressions, providing a more accurate reading of the person's emotions.

Step 3: Practice Active Observation

Active observation involves consciously paying attention to people's faces during interactions. Make a habit of noting facial expressions and correlating them with the person's spoken words and actions. This practice helps you become more attuned to subtle changes in expressions.

1. During conversations, glance at the person's face to observe their immediate reactions to your statements.
2. Note any discrepancies between their facial expressions and verbal responses, which might indicate underlying feelings not expressed in words.

Practice with a variety of people in different settings to improve your ability to read facial expressions accurately.

Step 4: Reflect and Validate

After observing facial expressions, reflect on your interpretations and validate them through feedback. If appropriate, ask the person how they feel to confirm your observations. This step not only helps you refine your skills but also demonstrates your attentiveness and empathy.

For example, if you notice a colleague frowning during a meeting, you might say, ***"I noticed you seem concerned about this point. Is there something specific on your mind?"*** This approach not only validates your observation but also opens up a dialogue for deeper understanding.

Step 5: Be Mindful of Cultural Differences

Cultural differences can influence how facial expressions are used and interpreted. Be mindful that certain expressions might vary across cultures, and consider these differences in your observations. When interacting with individuals from diverse backgrounds, be cautious in making assumptions based solely on facial expressions.

Understanding and interpreting facial expressions allows you to gauge how others are reacting to your communication, helping you adjust your approach to foster better interactions.

Noticing Gestures

Gestures are movements of the hands, arms, or other parts of the body that communicate a variety of messages. They can be intentional, such as waving or pointing, or unintentional, such as fidgeting or crossing arms.

How You Can Do It

Step 1: Understand Common Gestures and Their Meanings

Familiarize yourself with common gestures and their typical meanings. This foundational knowledge helps you interpret gestures more accurately during interactions.

- **Open Hand Gestures:** Indicate openness and honesty. For example, spreading hands apart with palms up can show that someone is being open and truthful.
- **Pointing:** Used to emphasize a point or direct attention. However, pointing directly at someone can be perceived as aggressive or rude.
- **Crossed Arms:** Often interpreted as a defensive or closed-off posture, though it can also indicate that someone is cold or thinking deeply.
- **Fidgeting:** This can suggest nervousness, boredom, or impatience. Common examples include tapping fingers, playing with objects, or shifting in the seat.
- **Steepling Fingers:** Bringing fingertips together in a steeple-like position can indicate confidence and self-assuredness.

Step 2: Observe the Context

The meaning of gestures can vary significantly depending on the context in which they are used. Pay attention to the surrounding situation, the person's verbal communication, and their overall body language to accurately interpret gestures.

For instance, crossed arms during a heated discussion might indicate defensiveness or disagreement, while crossed arms in a cold room might simply indicate that the person is trying to stay warm. Similarly, fidgeting during a presentation might suggest nervousness, whereas fidgeting during a long meeting might indicate restlessness or boredom.

Step 3: Practice Active Observation

Make a conscious effort to observe gestures during interactions. Focus on the person's hands and arms, and note any movements that stand out. Combining this with observing facial expressions and posture provides a comprehensive understanding of their non-verbal communication.

During conversations, notice if the person uses open or closed gestures. Open gestures can indicate that they are comfortable and engaged, while closed gestures might suggest they are feeling defensive or reserved.

Pay attention to repetitive gestures, such as tapping or fidgeting, which can indicate underlying emotions like anxiety or impatience.

Step 4: Interpret Clusters of Gestures

Gestures rarely occur in isolation; they are usually part of a cluster of non-verbal signals. Interpreting these clusters can provide a more accurate understanding of the person's feelings and intentions.

For example, if someone has their arms crossed, is leaning away, and has a frown, it collectively suggests they might be feeling defensive or disagreeing with what's being said. In contrast, if someone is leaning forward with open palms and nodding, it indicates interest and agreement.

Step 5: Reflect and Validate

After observing gestures, reflect on your interpretations and, if appropriate, validate them through feedback. This helps ensure that your interpretations are accurate and can improve your understanding of the person's non-verbal communication.

For example, if you notice a colleague frequently fidgeting during a meeting, you might follow up with them afterward to check-in. ***"I noticed you seemed a bit restless during the discussion. Is everything okay?"*** This approach not only validates your observation but also shows your attentiveness and concern.

Step 6: Consider Cultural Differences

Be aware that the meaning of gestures can vary across different cultures. A gesture that is positive in one culture might be considered rude or offensive in another. Understanding these cultural nuances is crucial for accurate interpretation in diverse settings.

For instance, while a thumbs-up gesture is a sign of approval in many Western cultures, it can be considered offensive in some Middle Eastern cultures. When interacting with people from different cultural backgrounds, be cautious in interpreting gestures and, when in doubt, seek clarification.

Gestures play a significant role in non-verbal communication, adding emphasis, indicating direction, expressing emotions, and complementing verbal messages. Noticing and interpreting gestures can provide deeper insights into a person's thoughts and feelings, often revealing more than words alone.

Interpreting Posture

Posture refers to the way we position our bodies when sitting, standing, or moving. It is a significant aspect of non-verbal communication that can convey a person's attitude, confidence level, openness, and emotional state.

How You Can Do It

Step 1: Recognize Common Postures and Their Implications

Familiarize yourself with common postures and what they typically signify. This foundational knowledge will help you interpret postural cues during interactions.

- **Open Posture:** Involves uncrossed arms and legs, a forward-facing body, and relaxed muscles. This posture usually indicates openness, receptiveness, and engagement. For instance, a person with an open posture during a meeting is likely interested and actively participating.
- **Closed Posture:** Characterized by crossed arms or legs, a turned-away body, and tense muscles. It often signals defensiveness, discomfort, or disinterest. For example, a person sitting with their arms crossed and their body turned away might be feeling defensive or uninterested in the conversation.
- **Leaning Forward:** Suggests interest and engagement. When someone leans towards you while speaking, it indicates they are attentive and involved in the discussion.

- **Leaning Back:** This can indicate relaxation but also disinterest or a desire to distance oneself from the conversation. The context and accompanying body language are crucial for accurate interpretation.
- **Slouching:** This may indicate a lack of confidence, boredom, or fatigue. A person who is slouching during a presentation might be disengaged or tired.
- **Erect Posture:** Conveys confidence and alertness. Standing or sitting straight with shoulders back typically signals that a person is confident and attentive.

Step 2: Observe the Context

The context in which a posture is observed greatly influences its interpretation. Pay attention to the environment, the ongoing conversation, and the overall body language to understand the context of the posture.

For example, someone might lean back and cross their arms during a casual conversation to signal relaxation, but the same posture during a heated debate might indicate defensiveness. Similarly, slouching might be acceptable and indicate relaxation in an informal setting but could signal disinterest in a professional meeting.

Step 3: Look for Consistency with Other Cues

Posture often works in conjunction with other non-verbal cues such as facial expressions, gestures, and tone of voice. Observing these cues together can provide a more accurate interpretation of a person's feelings and attitudes.

For instance, a person with an open posture, smiling face, and engaging tone of voice is likely to feel positive and receptive. Conversely, a closed posture combined with a frown and a monotone voice might indicate discomfort or resistance. Consistency among these cues reinforces the interpretation, making it more reliable.

Step 4: Reflect and Validate

Reflect on your observations of a person's posture and validate your interpretations when appropriate. Engaging in follow-up conversations can help confirm whether your interpretation was correct.

For example, if you notice a colleague with a closed posture during a discussion, you might later ask, *"I noticed you seemed a bit tense earlier. Is there something*

you'd like to talk about?" This validation not only confirms your observation but also shows that you are attentive and concerned.

Step 5: Consider Cultural and Individual Differences

Cultural and individual differences can significantly influence how postures are used and interpreted. What is considered open and positive in one culture might be perceived differently in another.

For instance, maintaining a straight posture with direct eye contact might be seen as confident in Western cultures but could be interpreted as aggressive or confrontational in some Asian cultures. Understanding these differences is crucial for accurate interpretation in diverse settings. Additionally, individual personality traits can influence postural habits, so it's important to consider the person's usual behavior when interpreting their posture.

Posture can indicate whether someone is relaxed or tense, engaged or disinterested, and open or defensive. Understanding and interpreting posture helps you gain insights into a person's feelings and attitudes, which can enhance your ability to communicate effectively and empathetically.

Understanding Eye Contact

Eye contact is a powerful form of non-verbal communication that can convey a wide range of emotions and intentions. It involves looking directly into someone's eyes during an interaction, which can signal attentiveness, interest, confidence, and sincerity. The frequency, duration, and intensity of eye contact can all influence how a message is perceived.

How You Can Do It

Step 1: Recognize the Functions of Eye Contact

Eye contact serves several important functions in communication:

- **Regulating Interaction:** Eye contact can signal when it is someone's turn to speak or listen. For example, during a conversation, people often look at their interlocutor to indicate that they are ready for a response.
- **Conveying Engagement and Interest:** Sustained eye contact shows that you are paying attention and interested in the interaction. It can make the other person feel valued and understood.

- **Expressing Emotions:** Eyes can convey emotions such as happiness, sadness, anger, or surprise. The context and accompanying facial expressions help determine the specific emotion.
- **Building Connection:** Maintaining appropriate eye contact helps build rapport and trust. It can make interactions feel more personal and sincere.

Step 2: Observe the Context of Eye Contact

The context in which eye contact occurs is crucial for accurate interpretation. Different situations and relationships can influence how eye contact is perceived.

- **Professional Settings:** In professional environments, steady eye contact often conveys confidence, competence, and attentiveness. However, it should not be overly intense, as this can come across as aggressive.
- **Social Settings:** In social interactions, eye contact helps create a connection and show empathy. It is important to balance eye contact with natural breaks to avoid making the other person uncomfortable.
- **Cultural Contexts:** Cultural norms play a significant role in how eye contact is used and interpreted. In some cultures, direct eye contact is seen as a sign of confidence and honesty, while in others, it may be considered disrespectful or confrontational.

Step 3: Interpret the Duration and Intensity

The duration and intensity of eye contact can provide additional insights into the other person's feelings and intentions:

- **Short Glances:** Brief eye contact can indicate curiosity or interest but might also suggest distraction or discomfort if it is too fleeting.
- **Prolonged Eye Contact:** Sustained eye contact usually signifies strong interest, engagement, or confidence. However, if it becomes too prolonged, it might be perceived as staring, which can make the other person uncomfortable.
- **Avoiding Eye Contact:** Lack of eye contact can indicate nervousness, discomfort, dishonesty, or disinterest. It is important to consider other non-verbal cues and the context to accurately interpret this behavior.

Step 4: Use Eye Contact Effectively

To use eye contact effectively in your own communication:

- **Maintain Balance:** Strive to maintain a balance between direct eye contact and natural breaks. Too little eye contact can make you seem disinterested, while too much can be perceived as intimidating.
- **Show Engagement:** Use eye contact to show that you are engaged and interested in the conversation. Look directly at the person when they are speaking, and nod occasionally to show understanding.
- **Be Natural:** Let your eye contact flow naturally with the conversation. Forced or overly deliberate eye contact can come across as insincere or awkward.
- **Adjust According to the Situation:** Tailor your eye contact to the specific context and relationship. In a professional presentation, maintain steady eye contact with your audience to convey confidence. In a casual conversation, use eye contact more flexibly to create a comfortable interaction.

Step 5: Reflect and Validate

Reflect on your use of eye contact and how others respond to it. Seek feedback from trusted colleagues or friends to improve your eye contact skills. Validating your observations through feedback helps you refine your ability to use eye contact effectively.

For instance, if you notice someone seems uncomfortable during a conversation, reflect on whether your eye contact might be too intense. Ask for feedback to understand how you can adjust your approach.

Understanding eye contact helps you interpret others' feelings and intentions and use your own eye contact effectively to enhance communication.

Analyzing Tone of Voice

The tone of voice refers to the way words are spoken, including the pitch, volume, pace, and intonation. It conveys emotions and attitudes beyond the literal meaning of the words.

How You Can Do It

Step 1: Recognize Key Elements of Tone

Understanding the key elements of tone of voice is the first step in analyzing it effectively:

- **Pitch:** The highness or lowness of the voice. High pitch can indicate excitement or anxiety, while low pitch often conveys seriousness or calmness.
- **Volume:** The loudness or softness of the voice. Loud volume can signify enthusiasm or anger, while soft volume may indicate shyness or intimacy.
- **Pace:** The speed at which someone speaks. Fast pace can suggest urgency or nervousness, while a slow pace often indicates thoughtfulness or hesitation.
- **Intonation:** The rise and fall of the voice. Rising intonation at the end of a sentence often signals a question or uncertainty, while falling intonation can indicate finality or confidence.

Step 2: Observe Consistency with Verbal and Non-Verbal Cues

Tone of voice should be considered in conjunction with the speaker's verbal content and other non-verbal cues such as body language and facial expressions. This holistic approach provides a clearer picture of the speaker's true emotions and intentions.

For example, if someone says, *"I'm fine,"* but their tone is flat, and their facial expression is tense, it's likely that they are not actually fine. Similarly, enthusiastic words delivered in a monotone voice may indicate insincerity.

Step 3: Pay Attention to Emotional Indicators

Tone of voice can reveal underlying emotions that the speaker may not be expressing explicitly:

- **Happiness:** Often characterized by a warm, upbeat tone, higher pitch, and varied intonation.
- **Anger:** Usually marked by a louder volume, faster pace, and more abrupt intonation.
- **Sadness:** Typically has a softer volume, slower pace, and lower pitch.
- **Nervousness:** Often indicated by a higher pitch, faster pace, and fluctuating intonation.

By paying attention to these indicators, you can better understand the emotional context of the conversation and respond empathetically.

Step 4: Consider Context and Relationship

The context of the conversation and your relationship with the speaker can influence the interpretation of their tone of voice. A tone that seems harsh in a formal setting might be normal in a casual one, and vice versa.

For example, a boss's firm tone during a performance review might be intended to convey seriousness and importance, while the same tone used during a casual office chat could come across as unnecessarily harsh. Similarly, a friend's teasing tone might be acceptable in a relaxed setting but inappropriate in a professional environment.

Step 5: Reflect and Validate

After interpreting the tone of voice, reflect on your observations and, if appropriate, validate them by seeking clarification from the speaker. This helps ensure that your interpretation is accurate and shows that you are attentive and concerned.

For instance, if you sense tension in a colleague's tone, you might say, ***"You sound a bit stressed. Is everything okay?"*** This validation not only confirms your interpretation but also opens up a dialogue for addressing any underlying issues.

Step 6: Practice and Seek Feedback

Practicing your ability to analyze tone of voice in various settings and seeking feedback from others can help improve this skill. Pay attention to how different tones are used in different contexts and how people react to them.

For example, during meetings or presentations, observe the tone of voice used by different speakers and the audience's reactions. Discuss your observations with trusted colleagues or mentors to gain insights and refine your ability to interpret tone accurately.

Analyzing tone of voice can provide insights into a speaker's true feelings and intentions, making it a crucial aspect of effective communication. Understanding and interpreting tone of voice helps you respond more appropriately and build stronger connections.

Effective communication in business involves mastering both verbal and non-verbal skills. By developing active listening, articulate speaking, and the ability to read and interpret non-verbal cues, you can significantly enhance your interactions, build stronger relationships, and achieve your professional goals.

Your communication skills are pivotal in shaping your professional success. By refining these skills, you can foster stronger relationships, inspire trust, and lead more effectively. Embrace continuous improvement in your communication approach, as it will empower you to navigate and thrive in any business environment.

CHAPTER 5: NETWORKING & RELATIONSHIP BUILDING

"Your network is your net worth."

– Porter Gale, Internationally Known Public Speaker, Networker, & Entrepreneur

Porter Gale's statement highlights the significant effect a strong professional network can have on career and business success. Establishing meaningful connections, engaging mentors, and cultivating long-term professional relationships are vital in unlocking growth across any industry. This chapter explores strategies for building and nurturing these essential bonds - so that networking becomes part of your professional journey rather than hindering it.

Networking in today's interconnected world means more than simply collecting contacts; it means forging meaningful relationships that lead to mutual growth and success. From industry events and professional associations to social media platforms and beyond, connecting and engaging with others is paramount for effective networking. Effective networking requires a combination of strategic outreach efforts, genuine interactions with individuals, and continued efforts at maintaining and deepening existing connections - by understanding and applying these principles, you can develop a network that upholds and advances your professional goals.

This chapter will take you step by step through networking, from building a strong professional network to using social media and connecting with mentors. You will discover practical methods and techniques for cultivating lasting relationships that provide long-term support and opportunities. By the time this chapter concludes, you will possess all of the tools required to successfully form and sustain networks that enhance professional growth and success.

Creating Meaningful Connections

Creating meaningful connections is essential for professional growth and success. These connections provide support, opportunities, and valuable insights that can propel your career forward. Building a strong professional network and leveraging social media for networking are two key strategies for developing these connections.

Building a Strong Professional Network

Building a strong professional network involves creating and maintaining relationships with individuals in your industry or related fields. These connections can offer support, resources, and opportunities that contribute to your professional growth and success. A robust network includes colleagues, mentors, industry leaders, and peers who can provide advice, collaborate on projects, and share valuable insights.

A professional network is crucial for several reasons:

1. **Access to Opportunities:** A strong network can open doors to job opportunities, collaborations, and partnerships.
2. **Knowledge Sharing:** Networking allows you to stay informed about industry trends, best practices, and new technologies.
3. **Support System:** A network provides a support system where you can seek advice, feedback, and encouragement.
4. **Career Advancement:** Connections with industry leaders and influencers can help you gain visibility and advance in your career.
5. **Personal Growth:** Engaging with a diverse group of professionals broadens your perspectives and enhances your personal and professional development.

Having a well-established professional network can significantly impact your career trajectory and overall success.

Tips on Building a Strong Professional Network

The following are some essential tips for building a strong professional network that can provide you with valuable support, opportunities, and insights throughout your career:

1. Attend Industry Events

Participating in industry conferences, seminars, and workshops is an excellent way to meet professionals in your field. These events provide opportunities to learn about the latest trends, exchange ideas, and establish new connections.

When attending these events, be proactive in introducing yourself to others. Prepare a brief introduction that highlights your background and interests. This will make it easier for you to engage in conversations and make a positive impression. For example, you could say, ***"Hi, I'm [Your Name], and I work in [Your Field/Industry]. I'm particularly interested in [Specific Aspect of Industry]."*** This introduction serves as an icebreaker and sets the stage for meaningful conversations.

Additionally, follow up with the contacts you make at these events. Send a quick email or LinkedIn message to express your appreciation for the conversation and suggest ways to stay in touch. This follow-up helps reinforce the connection and shows that you value the new relationship.

2. Join Professional Associations

Becoming a member of professional organizations related to your industry can expand your network. These associations often host networking events, webinars, and forums where you can meet peers and leaders in your field.

Engage actively with the organization by attending events, participating in discussions, and volunteering for committees or projects. This involvement not only helps you meet new people but also demonstrates your commitment to your profession. For example, if you join the American Marketing Association (AMA), you could volunteer to help organize a local chapter event, which would allow you to interact with other members and showcase your organizational skills.

Professional associations also provide access to exclusive resources, such as industry reports, job boards, and educational opportunities, which can further support your career development.

3. Leverage Networking Platforms

Use platforms like LinkedIn to connect with industry professionals. Join relevant groups, participate in discussions, and reach out to individuals whose work you admire.

Ensure your LinkedIn profile is comprehensive and professional, with a clear summary of your skills and experiences. Regularly update your profile with new achievements, skills, and endorsements to keep it current. Actively engaging with your network by posting articles, sharing industry news, and commenting on posts can help you stay visible and relevant.

When reaching out to new contacts, personalize your connection requests with a brief message explaining why you want to connect. For example, ***"Hi [Recipient's Name], I came across your profile and was impressed by your work in [Specific Area]. I'd love to connect and learn more about your experiences in [Industry/Field]."*** This personalized approach increases the likelihood of your request being accepted and sets the stage for meaningful interaction.

4. Volunteer for Projects and Committees

Volunteering for projects or committees within your organization or professional associations can help you build relationships with colleagues and industry peers. This involvement demonstrates your initiative and willingness to contribute beyond your immediate responsibilities.

For example, if your company is organizing a community outreach event, volunteering to lead a team or manage a project can showcase your leadership skills and allow you to work closely with colleagues from different departments. This collaboration helps build rapport and trust, which are essential for strong professional relationships.

Additionally, volunteering for industry-related initiatives, such as organizing a conference or contributing to a professional association's publication, can expand your network and increase your visibility in your field.

5. Follow Up and Maintain Connections

After meeting new contacts, follow up with them to maintain the relationship. Send a thank-you email, connect on LinkedIn, and periodically check in to stay in touch.

Regularly nurturing your network is crucial for its longevity and effectiveness. For instance, if you meet someone at a conference, send them a message within a few days to thank them for the conversation and suggest staying in touch. You could write, ***"It was great meeting you at [Event]. I enjoyed our discussion about [Topic]. Let's connect on LinkedIn and keep in touch."***

Maintain your connections by reaching out periodically to share updates, congratulate them on their achievements, or suggest meeting for coffee or lunch. These small gestures show that you value the relationship and are interested in maintaining it over time.

6. Offer Help and Support

Be willing to assist others in your network. Offering help when needed fosters goodwill and strengthens your connections.

For example, if a colleague is looking for a job, offer to review their resume or provide a referral if you know of relevant opportunities. Sharing resources, providing introductions, or offering your expertise on a topic can create a reciprocal relationship where both parties benefit.

Helping others not only builds strong relationships but also enhances your reputation as a reliable and supportive professional. This positive image can lead to further opportunities and connections in the future.

7. Express Gratitude

Acknowledging the support and contributions of your network members reinforces positive relationships. Simple acts of gratitude can go a long way in maintaining strong professional bonds.

Send thank-you notes or messages to express your appreciation for the help or advice you receive. For example, after a mentor provides guidance on a project, a thank-you email acknowledging their time and insights can strengthen the relationship. You could write, ***"Thank you so much for your invaluable advice on my project. Your insights were incredibly helpful, and I truly appreciate your support."***

By regularly expressing gratitude, you show that you value the contributions of your network, which encourages continued support and collaboration.

Building a strong professional network involves proactive efforts to connect, engage, and maintain relationships with individuals in your industry.

Leveraging Social Media for Networking

Social media is a powerful tool for building and maintaining professional relationships. It allows you to connect with a broad audience, share your expertise, and stay engaged with your network. By leveraging social media effectively, you can expand your reach, enhance your visibility, and create meaningful connections that support your professional growth.

Here is how you can do it:

Step 1: Create a Professional Profile

A well-crafted profile is the foundation of your social media presence. Ensure that your profile on various platforms reflects your professional accomplishments, skills, and goals.

What to Include:

- **Profile Picture:** Use a professional headshot that conveys confidence and approachability. A high-quality photo helps make a positive first impression. Avoid casual or low-quality images that may not reflect your professional demeanor.
- **Headline:** Write a clear, concise headline that summarizes your professional identity and key skills. For example, *"**Marketing Specialist | Content Creator | Digital Strategy Expert.**"* This headline should immediately convey your expertise and the value you bring.
- **Summary:** Craft a compelling summary that highlights your professional background, achievements, and career aspirations. This section should provide an overview of who you are and what you bring to the table. Mention key accomplishments, relevant skills, and your professional goals. Make sure it's engaging and tailored to attract the attention of potential connections and employers.

This clear and comprehensive profile makes it easier for others to understand your professional background and how you might collaborate or provide value.

Step 2: Share Valuable Content

Regularly posting valuable content is essential for establishing your expertise and engaging with your network. Share articles, write blog posts, and comment on industry news to demonstrate your knowledge and keep your profile active.

What to Share:

- **Industry Insights:** Share articles and insights about recent trends, technologies, or developments in your field. Providing valuable information helps position you as a thought leader and keeps your network informed.
- **Personal Achievements:** Post about your professional milestones, such as completing a major project, speaking at a conference, or receiving an award. Celebrating your successes not only highlights your accomplishments but also inspires and engages your audience.

- **Engaging Content:** Create and share content that sparks discussion and interaction. This could include thought-provoking questions, polls, or commentary on industry issues. Engaging content encourages your connections to interact with you, thereby strengthening your network.

For example, if you work in digital marketing, you might share a recent case study demonstrating the effectiveness of a new social media strategy. Accompany the post with insights about why the strategy worked and how others might apply similar techniques. This not only showcases your expertise but also provides practical value to your network.

Step 3: Engage with Your Network

Actively engaging with your connections is crucial for maintaining and strengthening relationships. Interaction through likes, comments, and shares shows that you are interested in others' contributions and helps keep your network vibrant.

How to Engage:

- **Comment Thoughtfully:** When commenting on posts, add meaningful insights or ask questions that contribute to the conversation. Generic comments like "Great post!" are less impactful than specific, thoughtful responses that show you've engaged with the content.
- **Share and Acknowledge:** Share posts from your connections and acknowledge their achievements. Congratulate them on their successes and provide encouragement. This reciprocity fosters goodwill and reinforces your relationships.
- **Participate in Groups and Discussions:** Join professional groups and participate in discussions relevant to your field. This involvement not only expands your network but also demonstrates your active participation in the industry.

For instance, if a connection posts about successful project completion, you could comment, *"Congratulations on the successful project! The strategy you implemented was particularly innovative. Can you share more about how you overcame the initial challenges?"* Such comments show genuine interest and encourage further dialogue.

Step 4: Join Relevant Groups and Discussions

Participating in groups and discussions on platforms like LinkedIn and Facebook allows you to connect with professionals who share your interests and goals. These groups provide a forum for networking, learning, and collaboration.

What to Look For:

- **Professional Groups:** Join groups that align with your industry, interests, or career goals. Look for active groups with regular discussions and a significant number of members. These groups can offer valuable networking opportunities and industry insights.
- **Discussion Forums:** Engage in discussion forums related to your field. Share your expertise, ask questions, and participate in conversations. This interaction helps you build a reputation as a knowledgeable and engaged professional.

How to Participate:

1. **Be Active and Consistent:** Regularly participate in group discussions by sharing insights, asking questions, and responding to others. Consistent participation helps you build visibility and credibility within the group.
2. **Provide Value:** Focus on adding value to the discussions. Share useful information, offer constructive feedback, and help others with their queries. Providing value not only enhances your reputation but also encourages others to reciprocate.

For example, if you are a member of a LinkedIn group for project managers, you might participate in discussions about best practices for managing remote teams. Sharing your experiences and tips can help others while positioning you as a knowledgeable and helpful member of the community.

Step 5: Use Social Media for Personal Branding

Use social media to build your personal brand by showcasing your expertise, values, and professional journey. Personal branding helps you stand out in your industry and attract opportunities.

What to Focus On:

- **Consistency:** Ensure consistency across all your social media profiles. Your branding should reflect your professional identity, values, and goals. Use the same profile picture, similar headlines, and consistent messaging across platforms.

- **Authenticity:** Be authentic in your posts and interactions. Share your genuine experiences, opinions, and insights. Authenticity helps build trust and makes your personal brand more relatable.
- **Professional Growth:** Highlight your professional growth by sharing learning experiences, new skills, and career milestones. Showcasing your continuous development demonstrates your commitment to your field.

How to Build Your Brand:

1. **Create Original Content:** Write articles, create videos, or develop infographics that showcase your expertise and insights. Original content sets you apart and adds unique value to your network.
2. **Engage with Industry Leaders:** Interact with industry leaders by commenting on their posts, sharing their content, and participating in discussions. Building relationships with influential professionals can enhance your visibility and credibility.
3. **Share Your Story:** Share your professional journey, including challenges and successes. Personal stories make your brand more relatable and engaging. For example, you might post about how you overcame a significant career challenge and the lessons you learned from the experience.

For example, if you are an aspiring entrepreneur, you could document your journey of starting a business, the challenges you faced, and how you overcame them. Sharing these experiences can inspire others and attract followers who are interested in your story and expertise.

By strategically using social media platforms, you can expand your reach, enhance your visibility, and create meaningful connections that support your professional growth and success. Embrace these strategies to build a robust and supportive professional network online.

Finding and Engaging Mentors

Finding and engaging mentors is a crucial aspect of professional growth and development. Mentors provide guidance, support, and valuable insights that can help you navigate your career path more effectively.

Mentorship is critical for several reasons:

1. Guidance and Advice

Mentors provide experienced guidance and advice, helping you navigate complex career decisions and challenges. Their insights are drawn from their own professional experiences, offering practical solutions and strategies that might not be immediately apparent to you.

For example, if you are considering a career transition, a mentor can help you evaluate the pros and cons, share your own experiences with similar transitions, and provide actionable advice on making the switch smoothly. Their perspective can save you from potential missteps and ensure a more informed decision-making process. Moreover, mentors can help you identify hidden opportunities within your current role or industry that you might not have considered, thereby expanding your career horizons.

2. Skill Development

Mentors can identify your strengths and weaknesses, offering tailored advice on how to improve and develop new skills. They can recommend resources such as books, courses, and workshops and even provide hands-on training or shadowing opportunities to help you gain practical experience.

For instance, if you need to improve your public speaking skills, a mentor who excels in this area might guide you through specific techniques, recommend speaking clubs like Toastmasters, or provide feedback on your presentations. This targeted skill development is invaluable for continuous professional growth and can significantly enhance your competencies in key areas.

3. Networking Opportunities

A mentor's extensive network can open doors to new connections, job opportunities, and partnerships. By introducing you to their contacts, mentors can help you expand your professional network, which can lead to valuable collaborations and career advancements.

For example, a mentor might introduce you to a potential employer or collaborator at a networking event or recommend you for a job opening within their network. These introductions can provide you with access to influential industry professionals and opportunities that might otherwise be difficult to obtain.

4. Career Advancement

Having a mentor can enhance your visibility within your organization and industry, potentially leading to promotions and new opportunities. Mentors can advocate for you, provide references, and help you navigate organizational politics, thereby facilitating your career progression.

For instance, a mentor might recommend you for a leadership development program or suggest you as a candidate for a high-profile project. Their endorsement can carry significant weight and help you stand out in a competitive environment, accelerating your career growth.

5. Personal Growth

Mentors provide a sounding board for your ideas and challenges, helping you grow both personally and professionally. They can offer perspectives on work-life balance, stress management, and other personal development areas, ensuring you maintain a healthy and fulfilling career.

For example, if you are struggling with work-related stress, a mentor can share their strategies for managing stress and maintaining a work-life balance. Their support and encouragement can help you develop resilience and a positive mindset, which are crucial for long-term success and well-being.

By leveraging the experience and support of a mentor, you can navigate your career more effectively, overcome challenges, and achieve your professional goals with greater confidence and insight. Embrace the benefits of mentorship to enhance your professional journey and unlock new opportunities for growth and success.

How to Connect with the Right Mentors

Connecting with the right mentors involves a strategic process that includes identifying potential mentors, reaching out effectively, building a strong relationship, and keeping them engaged. Each step requires thoughtful planning and execution to ensure a successful mentorship experience:

Step 1: Identify Potential Mentors

The first step in finding a mentor is to identify individuals who have the experience, skills, and qualities you admire. Look for people who have achieved success in areas that align with your career goals and who demonstrate a willingness to share their knowledge.

Where to Look:

- **Within Your Organization:** Identify senior colleagues or leaders who have the expertise you seek. They are often more accessible and can provide insights specific to your company.
- **Professional Associations:** Join industry-specific associations where experienced professionals often participate in mentorship programs. These associations often have formal mentoring programs that can match you with a mentor based on your goals and interests.
- **Networking Events:** Attend industry conferences, seminars, and meetups to connect with potential mentors. These events provide opportunities to meet industry leaders and professionals who can offer valuable insights and guidance.
- **Online Platforms:** Use platforms like LinkedIn to identify and reach out to professionals who inspire you. LinkedIn allows you to search for individuals based on their experience, skills, and industries, making it easier to find mentors who align with your career aspirations.

For instance, if you work in marketing and admire a senior executive's successful campaigns, consider approaching them for mentorship. Look for opportunities to interact with them at company events or through mutual connections. Additionally, reading industry publications and following thought leaders on social media can help you identify potential mentors.

Step 2: Reach Out with a Clear Request

When approaching a potential mentor, be clear about what you are seeking and why you think they can help. A well-thought-out request demonstrates your seriousness and respect for their time.

How You Can Do It:

1. Craft a Personalized Message

Explain who you are, why you admire their work, and what specific guidance you are seeking. Be concise and respectful of their time.

For example, you can write, *"Dear [Name], I have been following your work in [specific area] and am impressed by your achievements. As someone aspiring to [specific goal], I would greatly value your guidance and insights. Would you be open to a brief meeting to discuss [specific topics]? I understand you have a busy schedule, and I would be grateful for any time you could spare. Thank you for considering my request."*

This approach shows that you have done your research and are genuinely interested in their advice. It also demonstrates that you respect their time by being specific and concise.

2. Be Respectful and Flexible

Acknowledge their busy schedule and offer flexible meeting times. Showing respect for their time increases the likelihood of a positive response.

For instance, you might suggest multiple time slots for a meeting or offer to connect via phone or video call if that's more convenient for them. Phrasing such as, *"I am available at your convenience and can adjust my schedule to meet with you"* shows that you are considerate and accommodating.

By crafting a personalized and respectful message, you show that you have put thought into your request and value their potential mentorship.

Step 3: Build a Strong Relationship

Once you have connected with a mentor, focus on building a strong and mutually beneficial relationship. This involves regular communication, showing appreciation, and being open to feedback.

How you can do it:

1. Schedule Regular Check-Ins

Set up regular meetings to discuss your progress, challenges, and any new insights. Consistent communication keeps the relationship active and productive.

For example, you could suggest monthly or bi-monthly check-ins, depending on both your schedules. You might say, *"Can we schedule a monthly meeting to review my progress and discuss any new developments?"*

2. Be Prepared and Engaged

Come to each meeting with specific questions or topics to discuss. Show that you value their time by being prepared and engaged.

Prepare a list of questions or topics you want to cover in each meeting. For instance, ***"I have been working on [specific project] and would love your feedback on [specific aspect]."*** This preparation demonstrates your commitment to making the most of their guidance.

3. Show Appreciation

Express gratitude for their time and advice. A simple thank-you note or email can go a long way in showing your appreciation.

After each meeting, send a follow-up email thanking them for their insights and summarizing the key takeaways. For example, ***"Thank you for your valuable insights during our last meeting. Your advice on [specific topic] has been incredibly helpful."***

Building a strong relationship with your mentor ensures that they remain invested in your growth and development.

Step 4: Keep Your Mentor Engaged

Maintaining a mentor's engagement over time requires effort and genuine interaction. Show that you are implementing their advice and share the outcomes of their guidance.

How you can do it:

1. Provide Updates on Your Progress

Regularly update your mentor on how their advice has impacted your work. Sharing successes and lessons learned keeps them invested in your growth.

For instance, you could say, ***"Following your suggestion, I implemented [specific strategy] and saw [specific result]. Thank you for the guidance."***

2. Seek Their Opinion on New Challenges

Continuously seek their input on new challenges or decisions you face. This shows that you value their ongoing support and expertise.

For example, *"I am considering [new opportunity] and would love to hear your thoughts on the potential benefits and challenges."*

3. Involve Them in Your Successes

Invite your mentor to share in your successes, whether by attending a presentation you are giving or celebrating a milestone.

For instance, *"I will be presenting our new strategy at the upcoming meeting and would be honored if you could attend and provide your feedback."*

By keeping your mentor engaged and involved in your professional journey, you can maintain a productive and supportive relationship.

A well-chosen mentor can provide invaluable guidance and support, significantly enhancing your professional development and career success. Embrace these strategies to connect with mentors who can help you navigate your career journey with greater confidence and insight.

Maintaining Relationships

Building a professional network and finding mentors are critical steps for career growth, but maintaining these relationships over time is equally important. Strong, lasting relationships can provide continuous support, advice, and opportunities throughout your career.

Here are some tips for maintaining the professional relationships you've built:

1. Regularly Stay in Touch

Regularly staying in touch with your professional connections is essential for maintaining meaningful relationships. Consistent communication helps keep the relationship active and ensures that you remain relevant in each other's professional lives.

Here's how you can effectively stay in touch with your network:

- **Scheduled Check-Ins:** Setting reminders to check in with your contacts periodically can help you maintain regular communication. This could be through monthly or quarterly emails, phone calls, or even casual coffee meetings. Scheduling these interactions ensures that you don't lose touch over time and that your relationships remain strong. For example, you might set a reminder on your calendar to reach out to a key contact every three months, ensuring that your communication is consistent and timely.
- **Personalized Messages:** When you reach out, make your messages personal and specific. Referencing past conversations or shared experiences shows that you value the relationship and have a genuine interest in their life and career. Instead of sending generic messages, take the time to mention specific topics you've discussed before or ask about recent developments in your professional life. For instance, you could say, ***"Hi [Name], I remember you mentioned you were working on a new project last time we spoke. How's it going?"*** This personal touch makes your communication more meaningful and engaging.
- **Updates and Milestones:** Sharing your career milestones and seeking advice on new projects or challenges is a great way to keep your network informed and involved in your journey. Regular updates about your professional achievements, such as completing a significant project or starting a new role, provide conversation starters and opportunities for deeper engagement. For example, ***"Hi [Name], I wanted to share that I recently started a new position as [Your New Role]. I would love to catch up and hear your thoughts on my new responsibilities."*** This approach not only keeps your contacts informed about your progress but also invites them to share their insights and advice, reinforcing the connection.
- **Periodic Check-Ins:** Periodic check-ins don't always have to be about work. Sometimes, reaching out to simply ask how someone is doing can be equally valuable. This shows that you care about them as a person, not just as a professional contact. For instance, sending a message like, ***"Hi [Name], just wanted to check in and see how things are going with you. Hope all is well!"*** can help maintain a friendly and supportive relationship.
- **Leverage Technology:** Utilize technology to stay in touch more efficiently. Platforms like LinkedIn allow you to see updates and changes in your contacts' professional lives, providing natural opportunities to reach out. Congratulating someone on a new job or acknowledging a work anniversary can be a simple yet

effective way to stay connected. Additionally, using email scheduling tools can help you plan your communications in advance, ensuring that you maintain regular contact without needing to remember every detail manually.

- **Attend Events Together:** If possible, attending industry events, conferences, or seminars together can be a great way to maintain your relationship. Inviting your contacts to join you at such events provides an opportunity to catch up in person while also gaining new professional insights. For example, you could say, *"Hi [Name], I'm attending the [Event Name] next month. Would you be interested in joining me? It could be a great opportunity to catch up and discuss some of the latest industry trends."*
- **Consistent Engagement:** Engagement doesn't always have to be through direct messages. Consistently engaging with your contacts' social media posts, articles, or blogs by liking, commenting, and sharing their content can keep you on their radar. This kind of passive yet consistent interaction shows that you are interested in their work and supports maintaining a continuous presence in their professional life.

Regularly staying in touch with your professional network requires deliberate and thoughtful effort. Consistent engagement not only helps maintain your current network but also lays the groundwork for future opportunities and collaborations.

2. Show Appreciation and Acknowledge Contributions

Expressing gratitude and acknowledging the contributions of your professional contacts is essential for maintaining strong and positive relationships. Recognizing the support and assistance you receive not only reinforces the bond but also encourages ongoing collaboration and mutual respect.

Here's how you can effectively show appreciation and acknowledge contributions:

- **Thank-You Notes**

Sending thank-you notes or emails is a simple yet powerful way to express gratitude. After receiving help or advice, a quick thank-you message shows that you value the time and effort your contact has invested in you. Be specific about what you are thanking them for, and mention how their input has been beneficial.

For example, if a mentor provided you with guidance on a project, you might write, *"Dear [Name], thank you so much for your invaluable advice on the*

[specific project]. Your insights on [specific aspect] were incredibly helpful, and I truly appreciate your support." This specificity demonstrates that you paid attention to their input and valued their contribution.

- Public Acknowledgment

Acknowledging your contacts in public settings, such as on social media or during professional gatherings, can have a significant impact. Public acknowledgment boosts their visibility and reputation while also showing that you appreciate their efforts. For example, you could write a LinkedIn post highlighting the help you received, tagging the person, and briefly explaining how their advice or support made a difference.

An example of a LinkedIn post might be: "I want to extend my gratitude to [Name] for their incredible support and mentorship. Their guidance on [specific project or topic] was instrumental in achieving [specific outcome]. Thank you for being such an inspiring leader!" This not only shows appreciation but also provides them with positive exposure within your professional network.

- Gifts and Tokens of Appreciation

Occasionally, consider sending small tokens of appreciation to show your gratitude. These could be personalized gifts that reflect their interests or a simple gift card to their favorite coffee shop. The key is to choose something thoughtful that shows you have considered their preferences and contributions.

For instance, if your mentor loves reading, you might send a book related to your industry with a note saying, "I came across this book and thought you might enjoy it. Thank you for all your guidance and support!" Such gestures reinforce your appreciation in a tangible way.

- Consistent Acknowledgment

Make it a habit to consistently acknowledge the contributions of your contacts. Regular expressions of gratitude, whether through emails, messages, or public acknowledgments, ensure that your appreciation is ongoing rather than sporadic. This consistency helps build a positive and enduring relationship.

- Personal Touch

Adding a personal touch to your expressions of gratitude can make them more meaningful. Mentioning specific details or memories related to their help can enhance the sincerity of your message. For instance, "I still remember the advice you gave me during our first meeting about [specific topic]. It has truly shaped my approach to [specific area]. Thank you for always being there to guide me."

Showing appreciation and acknowledging contributions are crucial for maintaining strong professional relationships. By demonstrating your appreciation regularly and sincerely, you foster a supportive and collaborative professional network that benefits both you and your connections.

3. Be a Resource and Offer Help

Reciprocity is a cornerstone of strong professional relationships. Being a resource and offering help to your contacts not only strengthens your bond but also fosters a culture of mutual support and collaboration.

Here's how you can effectively be a resource and offer help to your professional network:

- **Share Opportunities**

Actively sharing opportunities with your contacts can greatly enhance your relationships. Whether it's job openings, professional events, or useful resources, providing information that could benefit your network shows that you are invested in their success.

For example, if you come across a job posting that fits someone's skills, forward it to them with a note: ***"Hi [Name], I saw this job opening at [Company] and thought it might be a great fit for you given your background in [Specific Field]. Hope it helps!"*** This proactive approach demonstrates that you are thinking about their career growth and are willing to support them.

- **Provide Introductions**

Facilitating introductions between your contacts can create new opportunities and strengthen your network if you know two people who could mutually benefit from knowing each other, take the initiative to introduce them.

For instance, *"Hi [Name1] and [Name2], I wanted to introduce you both as I believe you could collaborate on [specific area]. [Name1], [Name2] has extensive experience in [field], and [Name2], [Name1] has been working on some exciting projects in [related field]. I think you two would have a lot to discuss and potentially work together on."* This gesture not only helps your contacts but also positions you as a connector within your network.

- **Volunteer Your Skills**

Offering your expertise and skills can be incredibly valuable to your contacts. Whether it's reviewing a document, providing feedback on a project, or sharing your knowledge on a specific topic, your willingness to help can foster deeper connections.

For example, *"Hi [Name], I noticed you're working on a new marketing strategy. I'd be happy to take a look and provide some feedback if that would be helpful. I've worked on similar projects and would love to share my insights."* By volunteering your skills, you show that you are willing to invest your time and effort to support their success.

- **Be Responsive**

Timely responses to requests for help or advice are crucial. When your contacts reach out to you, make it a priority to respond promptly and thoughtfully. This responsiveness demonstrates your reliability and commitment to maintaining a supportive relationship.

For instance, if a colleague asks for your input on a proposal, try to provide your feedback as soon as possible with detailed and constructive suggestions. *"Hi [Name], thanks for sharing your proposal. Here are some thoughts and suggestions that might help. Let me know if you need any further input."*

- **Offer to Collaborate**

Suggesting collaborations on projects or initiatives can be a great way to offer help while also benefiting from the experience. Collaborative efforts often lead to mutual learning and stronger professional bonds.

For example, *"Hi [Name], I'm working on a new project related to [specific topic] and thought you might be interested in collaborating. Your expertise in [related area] would be invaluable, and I think we could achieve great results together. Let's discuss this further if you're interested."* This not only offers them an opportunity but also opens up avenues for deeper professional engagement.

- **Share Your Network**

Introduce your contacts to your wider network whenever relevant. If someone is looking for expertise or connections in a specific area, and you know someone who can help, make the connection.

For example, *"Hi [Name], I know you're looking for insights into [specific area]. I'd like to introduce you to [Contact's Name], who has extensive experience in this field. I think you two could have a valuable conversation."* By sharing your network, you provide additional resources and support, enhancing your contacts' opportunities for growth.

- **Consistently Offer Help**

Make it a habit to regularly offer help without waiting for a request. Keep an eye out for ways you can support your contacts in their professional endeavors. This could be as simple as sending an article that might interest them or offering to review a document they're working on.

For instance, *"Hi [Name], I came across this article on [specific topic] and thought you might find it useful given your current project. Let me know if you want to discuss it further."* Such gestures show that you are consistently thinking about their success and are willing to contribute whenever possible.

Being a resource and offering help to your professional contacts fosters a culture of mutual support and collaboration. Consistent and proactive support demonstrates your commitment to your network's success and creates a foundation of trust and goodwill that benefits everyone involved.

4. Respect Their Time and Boundaries

Respecting the time and boundaries of your professional contacts is crucial for maintaining healthy and sustainable relationships. Being considerate of their schedules and personal limits demonstrates professionalism and fosters mutual respect.

Here's how you can effectively respect the time and boundaries of your network:

• **Be Considerate with Communication**

When reaching out to your contacts, ensure your messages are concise and to the point. Respect their time by clearly stating the purpose of your communication and avoiding unnecessary details. This approach shows that you value their time and are mindful of their busy schedules.

For example, if you need advice on a project, your email might read, *"Hi [Name], I hope you're well. I'm working on a project related to [specific topic] and would appreciate your insights on [specific question]. Any advice you could share would be incredibly valuable. Thank you!"* This concise message respects their time while clearly communicating your request.

• **Schedule Wisely**

When requesting meetings or calls, propose flexible scheduling options that accommodate their availability. Offer several time slots and be willing to adjust based on their preferences. Confirm appointments in advance and avoid last-minute changes, as this can be disruptive and inconsiderate.

For instance, you could say, *"Could we schedule a call to discuss this further? I'm available on Monday and Wednesday between 2-4 PM, but I'm happy to adjust to a time that suits you better. Please let me know what works best for you."* Providing options and expressing flexibility shows respect for their schedule.

• **Understand Boundaries**

Recognize and respect the personal and professional boundaries of your contacts. Avoid over-communicating or reaching out during inappropriate times, such as late at night or during weekends, unless it's urgent and they've indicated it's acceptable.

For example, if you know a colleague who prefers not to discuss work outside office hours, make sure to honor that preference. If an urgent situation arises, you might preface your message with, ***"I apologize for reaching out outside of regular hours, but I need your urgent input on [specific issue]. Thank you for understanding."***

• Respect Their Time

Be punctual and prepared for meetings and calls. Arriving on time and having a clear agenda demonstrates that you respect their time and are serious about the interaction. Avoid wasting time with small talk when the purpose of the meeting is clear and important.

For example, when attending a scheduled meeting, ensure you are ready with any necessary documents or questions. Starting with, ***"Thank you for taking the time to meet with me today. I'd like to discuss [specific topics] and get your feedback on [specific issues],"*** shows that you are organized and respectful of their time.

• Limit Frequency of Requests

Avoid bombarding your contacts with frequent requests for help or advice. Space out your interactions and ensure that each request is meaningful and necessary. Over-relying on contact can strain the relationship and make them less willing to assist in the future.

For example, if you've recently asked for their input on a project, give them time before making another request. Instead, update them on how their previous advice was implemented and the results it achieved. This balance ensures you don't overstep and maintain a respectful relationship.

• Acknowledge Their Limits

Be mindful that your contacts may have their own commitments and limitations. If they decline a request or need more time to respond, respect their decision without pressuring them. Acknowledge their constraints and show understanding.

For instance, if a mentor declines a meeting due to a busy schedule, respond with, ***"I completely understand and appreciate your time. Please let me know when you're available, and we can reschedule. Thank you!"*** This response shows empathy and respect for their situation.

• Provide Context

When reaching out, provide enough context so that your contact can understand your request without needing additional information. This efficiency respects their time and makes it easier for them to assist you.

For example, ***"I'm working on a presentation about [specific topic] and would love your insights on [specific aspect]. The slides I've prepared so far are attached. Could you review them and provide feedback?"*** This clear context helps them quickly grasp your needs and offer relevant assistance.

• Follow Up Thoughtfully

If you haven't received a response, follow up politely without being intrusive. Allow a reasonable amount of time before sending a follow-up message, and keep it courteous and understanding.

For instance, ***"Hi [Name], I wanted to follow up on my previous email regarding [specific request]. I understand you're busy, so please take your time. Any feedback you can provide would be greatly appreciated. Thank you!"*** This respectful follow-up shows that you value their time and patience.

Respecting the time and boundaries of your professional contacts is fundamental to maintaining strong and respectful relationships. These practices ensure that your interactions remain positive, productive, and sustainable, benefiting both you and your professional network.

Maintaining professional relationships requires ongoing effort, genuine engagement, and mutual respect. By consistently nurturing these connections, you create a supportive network that can provide invaluable resources and opportunities throughout your career.

CHAPTER 6: LEADERSHIP AND INFLUENCE

"Leadership is not about being in charge. It is about taking care of those in your charge."

– Simon Sinek, English American Author & Inspirational Speaker

The words of Simon Sinek describe leadership in a nutshell: it is to serve people. First of all, leadership is not limited to the power of control or domination; it concerns giving guidance when needed to enable a subordinate to reach his utmost potential. This chapter elaborates on the qualities of a leader, how to win team support and inspire them, games played by brain in winning agreement, and much more. These principles are then extended into practical ways for developing leadership skills that will promote your success as well as the establishment of a sound organizational culture.

Today, leadership holds greater relevance than ever before in a business environment that is constantly evolving. Leadership is not only steering the ship but also identifying and fulfilling the needs of the crew. Skills one must develop include vision, emotional intelligence, decision-making skills, flexibility, integrity, communicative abilities, assertiveness, safety understanding, know-how value, and perseverance. It falls upon you to develop these attributes within your team members so that they can overcome those challenges standing in the way of achieving common goals. This chapter gives you tools and teachings regarding how to lead with purposeful missions and to measure a positive atmosphere amongst your team players.

Leadership also involves the power to influence people, which is crucial for the accomplishment of organizational objectives and for creating a positive working environment. Persuasion does not only come through changing people's opinions but also through earning their confidence, identifying mutual values, and giving arguments that are free from bias. If you are closing a deal, trying to get your employees on board with an initiative, or effecting a change, the ability to influence can be a great difference maker. This chapter will provide you with the skills and techniques that will serve as your asset in upgrading your persuasive skills for leading in an effective and ethical manner. At the end of this chapter, you are on the verge of being able to herd your team toward ideas that benefit the collective.

Developing Leadership Qualities

Your ability to lead effectively hinges on developing certain key traits and continuously enhancing your leadership skills. Whether you're an emerging leader or an experienced one, focusing on these aspects will help you guide your team more successfully and foster a positive work environment.

Key Traits of Effective Leaders

The following are some key traits of effective leaders you can cultivate to enhance your leadership abilities and drive success within your organization:

1. **Vision and Clarity:** Effective leaders have a clear vision of where they want to take their organization. As discussed previously, your vision should not only outline your long-term goals but also provide a roadmap for achieving them. A well-articulated vision inspires and motivates your team, helping them understand the bigger picture and their role in it. This clarity in direction ensures that all team members are aligned and working towards common objectives, fostering a sense of purpose and unity.
2. **Emotional Intelligence:** Emotional intelligence (EI) is the ability to understand and manage your own emotions while recognizing and influencing the emotions of others. Leaders with high EI are adept at navigating social complexities, leading with empathy, and maintaining positive relationships. They can handle stress, communicate effectively, and defuse conflicts, creating a harmonious and productive work environment. Emotional intelligence is crucial for building trust and respect, which are foundational for effective leadership.
3. **Decisiveness:** Decisiveness involves making timely and confident decisions, often in the face of uncertainty. Effective leaders gather relevant information, weigh their options, and take decisive action. This ability is critical for maintaining momentum and ensuring that opportunities are seized promptly. Decisiveness also demonstrates a leader's confidence and reliability, encouraging their team to trust in their judgment and follow their lead without hesitation.
4. **Adaptability:** Adaptability is the capacity to adjust to new conditions and respond effectively to change. In a constantly evolving business landscape, leaders must be flexible and open to new ideas and approaches. Adaptable leaders can pivot strategies as needed, address unexpected challenges, and capitalize on emerging opportunities. This trait ensures that the organization remains resilient and competitive in the face of external pressures and internal shifts.
5. **Integrity:** Integrity involves being honest, ethical, and consistent in your actions and decisions. Leaders with integrity build credibility and trust, which are essential for fostering a culture of accountability and respect within the organization. They lead by example, uphold their commitments, and make decisions based on ethical considerations rather than convenience. Integrity is

not only a moral imperative but also a strategic advantage, as it strengthens the leader's reputation and the organization's ethical foundation.
6. **Communication Skills:** Effective communication is fundamental to leadership. Leaders must convey their ideas clearly and persuasively, ensuring that their message is understood and embraced by their team. This includes not only verbal and written communication but also non-verbal cues and active listening. Strong communication skills help leaders articulate their vision, provide constructive feedback, and foster an open and inclusive dialogue within the team.
7. **Confidence:** Confidence is the belief in one's abilities and judgment. Confident leaders inspire trust and instill confidence in their team. They are willing to take risks, make bold decisions, and stand by their choices. Confidence is not about arrogance but about having a balanced sense of self-assurance grounded in competence and experience. This trait helps leaders navigate challenges with poise and resilience, motivating their team to remain focused and committed.
8. **Empathy:** Empathy is the ability to understand and share the feelings of others. Empathetic leaders are attuned to their team members' needs and concerns, fostering a supportive and inclusive environment. By showing genuine care and understanding, they build stronger relationships and enhance team morale. Empathy also enables leaders to make more informed and compassionate decisions, which can improve overall organizational health and employee satisfaction.
9. **Accountability:** Accountability involves taking responsibility for one's actions and decisions. Effective leaders hold themselves and their team accountable for their performance and outcomes. This trait ensures that standards are maintained, goals are met, and any issues are promptly addressed. By promoting a culture of accountability, leaders encourage a sense of ownership and commitment within their team, driving higher levels of performance and integrity.
10. **Resilience:** Resilience is the ability to recover from setbacks and persist in the face of adversity. Resilient leaders maintain their focus and determination even during challenging times. They view obstacles as opportunities for growth and learning, fostering a positive and proactive mindset within their team. Resilience is crucial for sustaining long-term success and navigating the inevitable ups and downs of business.

These key traits of effective leaders are essential for guiding teams, driving organizational success, and fostering a positive work culture. By embodying these characteristics, you can enhance your leadership abilities and make a meaningful impact within your organization.

Exercises to Enhance Leadership Skills

Developing leadership skills requires ongoing practice and reflection.

Here are some exercises designed to enhance various aspects of leadership:

1. Vision Board Creation

Creating a vision board is a powerful exercise that helps you clarify your goals and visualize your future. It serves as a tangible representation of your aspirations and the steps needed to achieve them. A vision board not only provides direction but also acts as a constant reminder of your ambitions, keeping you motivated and focused.

Here's how you can create an effective vision board:

Step 1: Gather Materials

The first step in creating a vision board is to gather all the necessary materials. This process can be both fun and inspiring, as it allows you to explore various sources for visual and textual content that resonates with your goals.

Start by collecting magazines, printed images, and quotes that inspire you. These can be from various domains such as career, personal growth, health, and relationships. Ensure that you have a variety of materials to choose from, as this will help create a diverse and comprehensive vision board. You can also look for specific themes or keywords that align with your goals to keep your vision board focused and relevant.

In addition to printed materials, gather tools such as scissors, glue, markers, and a large sheet of paper or a corkboard. These tools will help you cut out, arrange, and affix your chosen images and quotes. Consider also including personal photographs or mementos that hold special significance to you. These personal touches can make your vision board more meaningful and unique to your aspirations.

Finally, create a dedicated space for your vision board where you can work on it without interruptions. This could be a quiet corner of your home or office where you can focus on your goals and reflect on your aspirations. Having a dedicated space will help you immerse yourself in the process and create a vision board that truly reflects your dreams and desires.

Step 2: Reflect on Your Goals

Before you start assembling your vision board, take some time to reflect on your personal and professional goals. This reflection process is crucial as it helps you identify what you truly want to achieve and the steps needed to get there.

Begin by asking yourself key questions about your aspirations:

- What do you want to accomplish in your career?
- What personal goals do you have for your health, relationships, and personal growth?

Write down your answers and prioritize them based on their importance and feasibility. This exercise will help you gain clarity on your objectives and ensure that your vision board is aligned with your most important goals.

Consider breaking down your goals into short-term and long-term categories. Short-term goals might include things you want to achieve within the next year, while long-term goals could span several years or even decades. By categorizing your goals, you can create a balanced vision board that addresses both immediate and future aspirations.

Reflecting on your goals also involves visualizing the steps needed to achieve them. Think about the actions you need to take, the resources you require, and the support systems that can help you along the way. This detailed reflection will provide a solid foundation for your vision board and ensure that it serves as a practical guide to achieving your dreams.

Step 3: Select Images and Quotes

Once you have a clear understanding of your goals, it's time to select images and quotes that resonate with your vision. This step involves curating content that inspires and motivates you, reflecting the essence of your aspirations.

Browse through the magazines, printed materials, and online resources you gathered earlier. Look for images that symbolize your goals and the emotions associated with achieving them. For example, if one of your goals is to become a successful entrepreneur, you might choose images of thriving businesses, confident business leaders, and symbols of success like awards or financial growth. The images should evoke a strong emotional response, making you feel excited and motivated about your goals.

In addition to images, select quotes that inspire and uplift you. These quotes can be from famous leaders, authors, or even personal mentors. The key is to choose words that resonate with your values and aspirations. For instance, a quote like ***"The only way to do great work is to love what you do"*** by Steve Jobs might inspire you to pursue your passion with dedication and enthusiasm.

As you select images and quotes, consider the layout and design of your vision board. Think about how you want to arrange the content to create a visually appealing and coherent representation of your goals. This planning will help you create a vision board that is not only inspiring but also aesthetically pleasing.

Step 4: Arrange and Affix Your Content

With your images and quotes selected, the next step is to arrange and affix them to your board. This step involves organizing your content in a way that reflects your goals and aspirations clearly and compellingly.

Start by laying out all your selected images and quotes on the board without gluing them down. Experiment with different arrangements to see what looks best and feels most inspiring to you. Consider grouping related images and quotes together to create thematic sections, such as career goals, personal growth, health, and relationships. This organization can help you focus on different aspects of your life and ensure that your vision board is comprehensive and balanced.

Once you are satisfied with the arrangement, start gluing the images and quotes onto the board. Use markers or decorative elements to highlight key areas or add personal touches. For example, you might draw arrows or circles around particularly important goals or add stickers and washi tape to enhance the visual appeal. The process should be creative and enjoyable, allowing you to engage with your aspirations on a deeper level.

As you affix your content, take the time to reflect on each goal and visualize yourself achieving it. This visualization reinforces your commitment and helps embed your goals in your subconscious mind, making you more likely to take the necessary actions to achieve them.

Step 5: Place Your Vision Board Prominently

After completing your vision board, place it somewhere you will see it regularly. This step is crucial as it ensures that your goals remain at the top of your mind and continue to inspire you daily.

Choose a location where you spend a lot of time, such as your office, bedroom, or study area. The key is to place the vision board in a spot where you will see it frequently, reminding you of your goals and keeping you motivated. For example, if you place it in your office, it will serve as a constant reminder of what you are working towards and help you stay focused during your workday.

Make it a habit to spend a few moments each day looking at your vision board and reflecting on your goals. Visualize yourself achieving each goal and feel the emotions associated with your success. This daily practice can boost your motivation and reinforce your commitment to your aspirations.

Step 6: Review and Update Regularly

A vision board is not a static tool; it should evolve as your goals and circumstances change. Regularly reviewing and updating your vision board ensures that it remains relevant and aligned with your current aspirations.

Set aside time every few months to review your vision board. Reflect on your progress and assess whether your goals have changed or new aspirations have emerged. Remove images and quotes that no longer resonate with you and add new ones that reflect your updated goals. This process keeps your vision board dynamic and ensures that it continues to inspire and guide you effectively.

Updating your vision board also involves celebrating your achievements. When you accomplish a goal, take a moment to acknowledge your success and reflect on the journey. Consider adding a new section to your vision board to highlight your accomplishments, serving as a reminder of what you have achieved and motivating you to reach even higher.

Creating a vision board is a powerful exercise that helps you visualize your goals and stay focused on your aspirations. Embrace this creative process to enhance your clarity, commitment, and success in achieving your dreams.

2. Emotional Intelligence Journaling

Developing high emotional intelligence is essential for effective leadership, as it enhances your ability to connect with your team, navigate social complexities, and create a positive work environment. Emotional intelligence journaling is a powerful tool that can help you improve your EI by fostering greater self-awareness and emotional regulation.

Here is how you can do this:

Step 1: Dedicate Time for Daily Journaling

To begin emotional intelligence journaling, set aside dedicated time each day for this practice. Consistency is key to reaping the benefits of journaling, so choose a time that works best for you, whether it's in the morning, during a lunch break, or before bed.

Start by finding a quiet and comfortable space where you can reflect without distractions. Ensure you have a journal or a digital device where you can write your thoughts and experiences. Establishing a routine for journaling helps integrate this practice into your daily life, making it a regular part of your self-improvement efforts.

Begin each session by reflecting on your day and noting any significant events or interactions that impacted you emotionally. Describe these events in detail, focusing on what happened, how you felt, and how you responded. This exercise helps you become more aware of your emotional triggers and patterns, providing valuable insights into your emotional landscape.

Step 2: Reflect on Specific Interactions

Focusing on specific interactions can help you better understand how your emotions influence your behavior and how you affect others. By examining these interactions, you can identify areas where you handled situations well and areas where you could improve.

Choose a particular interaction from your day that stood out to you, either because it was positive or challenging. Reflect on the emotions you experienced during this interaction.

Ask yourself questions like:

- What emotions did I feel?
- Why did I feel this way?
- How did my emotions influence my behavior?
- How did the other person react?

Answering these questions can help you gain deeper insights into your emotional responses and their impact on others.

For example, if you had a difficult conversation with a colleague, write about the emotions you felt before, during, and after the conversation. Describe how you managed these emotions and how the conversation unfolded. Reflect on what you did well and what you could have done differently to improve the outcome. This detailed analysis helps you build emotional intelligence by learning from your experiences.

Step 3: Identify Patterns and Triggers

As you continue journaling, look for patterns and triggers in your emotions and behavior. Identifying these patterns can help you anticipate and manage your emotional responses more effectively, leading to better emotional regulation and decision-making.

Review your journal entries regularly, paying attention to recurring themes and emotional triggers.

- *Are there specific situations or people that consistently evoke strong emotions?*
- *How do these emotions affect your behavior and interactions?*

Recognizing these patterns allows you to develop strategies for managing your emotions more effectively.

For instance, you might notice that you feel anxious before important meetings and that this anxiety affects your confidence and communication. With this awareness, you can develop coping mechanisms, such as deep breathing exercises or positive self-talk, to manage your anxiety and perform better in these situations. By understanding your emotional triggers, you can take proactive steps to regulate your emotions and improve your interactions.

Step 4: Practice Empathy and Perspective-Taking

Emotional intelligence involves not only understanding your own emotions but also recognizing and empathizing with the emotions of others. Journaling can help you practice empathy by encouraging you to see situations from different perspectives.

When reflecting on interactions in your journal, consider the emotions and perspectives of the other people involved.

Ask yourself questions like:

- *How might the other person have felt during this interaction?*
- *What factors could have influenced their behavior?*
- *How could I have responded more empathetically?*

Practicing perspective-taking helps you develop a deeper understanding of others' emotions and improves your ability to connect with and support them.

For example, if you have a disagreement with a team member, try to put yourself in their shoes and understand their point of view. Reflect on how you could have acknowledged their feelings and addressed their concerns more effectively. This practice fosters empathy and strengthens your relationships by showing that you value and respect others' perspectives.

Step 5: Set Emotional Intelligence Goals

Setting specific goals for improving your emotional intelligence can help you stay focused and motivated in your journaling practice. These goals should be realistic, measurable, and aligned with your overall leadership development objectives.

Identify areas of emotional intelligence you want to improve, such as emotional regulation, empathy, or conflict resolution. Set clear and actionable goals, such as "I will practice deep breathing exercises before meetings to manage my anxiety" or "I will actively listen and validate my team members' feelings during discussions." Write these goals in your journal and track your progress regularly.

Review your goals periodically to assess your progress and make adjustments as needed. Celebrate your achievements and reflect on the challenges you encountered. Setting and tracking emotional intelligence goals helps you stay committed to your development and provides a sense of accomplishment as you grow as a leader.

Step 6: Reflect and Review Regularly

Regular reflection and review of your journal entries are essential for continuous improvement. Set aside time each week or month to revisit your entries, assess your progress, and identify areas for further growth.

During these review sessions, look for patterns and trends in your emotional responses and interactions. Reflect on your successes and challenges, and consider what you have learned from your journaling practice. Use this reflection to refine your emotional intelligence goals and develop new strategies for managing your emotions and enhancing your interactions.

For example, if you notice that you have made significant progress in managing your anxiety during meetings, acknowledge this achievement and identify what strategies worked best for you. If you encounter recurring challenges, explore new approaches to address them. Regular reflection and review ensure that your journaling practice remains dynamic and effective, helping you continuously develop your emotional intelligence.

Emotional intelligence journaling is a powerful tool for developing self-awareness, emotional regulation, and empathy. Embrace this practice to deepen your understanding of your emotions and improve your ability to connect with and support others in your professional and personal life.

3. Decision-Making Simulations

Decision-making simulations are a practical tool for enhancing your ability to make effective decisions quickly and confidently. These exercises involve working through hypothetical scenarios that mimic real-life situations, allowing you to practice and refine your decision-making skills in a controlled environment.

Step 1: Create or Find Relevant Scenarios

The first step in decision-making simulations is to create or find scenarios that are relevant to your industry or role. These scenarios should reflect the types of decisions you are likely to encounter in your professional life, ranging from strategic business decisions to everyday operational choices.

Begin by identifying common challenges and decisions faced in your field. For example, if you are a project manager, scenarios might include dealing with resource constraints, managing project timelines, or resolving team conflicts. If you are an entrepreneur, scenarios might involve making investment decisions, launching new products, or navigating market competition.

You can create your scenarios based on your experiences and observations or use existing case studies and examples from industry literature. Ensure that each scenario is detailed and realistic, providing enough information to analyze the situation and make informed decisions.

Step 2: Analyze the Scenario

Once you have your scenarios, the next step is to analyze each one thoroughly. This involves gathering and evaluating all relevant information, identifying key issues, and considering the potential impacts of different decisions.

Start by carefully reading through the scenario and identifying the main problem or decision point. Break down the information provided, noting any constraints, opportunities, and critical factors that could influence your decision.

Ask yourself questions like:

- *What are the main objectives?*
- *What resources are available?*
- *What risks need to be managed?*

For example, if the scenario involves deciding whether to launch a new product, you might consider factors such as market demand, competitor actions, production costs, and potential revenue. Analyzing these elements helps you build a comprehensive understanding of the situation, which is essential for making informed decisions.

Step 3: Generate Possible Solutions

After analyzing the scenario, brainstorm possible solutions or courses of action. This step involves thinking creatively and considering multiple perspectives to identify a range of options.

List all the potential solutions, no matter how unconventional they might seem. Consider the pros and cons of each option, evaluating how well they address the main problem and align with your objectives. Be sure to think through the short-term and long-term implications of each choice, as well as any potential unintended consequences.

For instance, if you are deciding on a new marketing strategy, possible solutions might include:

- Launching a social media campaign.
- Partnering with influencers.
- Increasing advertising spending.
- Focusing on content marketing.

Evaluate each option based on factors such as reach, cost, and alignment with your brand values.

Step 4: Make a Decision

With a list of possible solutions, it's time to make a decision. Choose the option that best addresses the problem, aligns with your goals, and offers the most favorable balance of benefits and risks.

When making your decision, consider the following:

- **Alignment with Objectives:** Does the chosen solution align with your overall goals and strategy?
- **Feasibility:** Is the solution practical and achievable given your resources and constraints?
- **Risk Management:** How do the risks associated with the solution compare to the potential benefits?

For example, if you decide to launch a social media campaign, ensure that it aligns with your brand's objectives, is feasible within your budget, and effectively mitigates potential risks such as negative feedback or low engagement.

Step 5: Reflect on the Decision-Making Process

Reflection is a crucial part of decision-making simulations. After making a decision, take time to reflect on the process and evaluate the outcomes. This reflection helps you understand what worked well and what could be improved, enhancing your decision-making skills over time.

Consider the following questions during your reflection:
- What were the key factors that influenced your decision?
- Were there any biases or assumptions that affected your judgment?
- How could the decision-making process be improved in future scenarios?

For instance, if you found that certain biases influenced your decision, think about strategies to mitigate these biases in the future. This might involve seeking diverse perspectives, using decision-making frameworks, or developing a more structured approach to evaluating options.

Step 6: Discuss with a Mentor or Peer

Discussing your decision-making simulations with a mentor or peer can provide valuable feedback and additional insights. Sharing your thought process and outcomes allows you to gain different perspectives and learn from others' experiences.

Choose a mentor or peer who has relevant experience and can offer constructive feedback. Walk them through the scenario, your analysis, the options you considered, and the final decision you made. Encourage them to ask questions and provide suggestions for improvement.

For example, your mentor might point out alternative solutions you hadn't considered or highlight potential risks that you overlooked. This feedback helps you refine your decision-making approach and prepares you for real-life situations.

Step 7: Apply Lessons Learned to Real-Life Situations

The ultimate goal of decision-making simulations is to apply the lessons learned to real-life situations. Use the insights and skills gained from these exercises to enhance your decision-making in your professional life.

Reflect on how the simulations have improved your ability to analyze information, generate solutions, and make confident decisions. Consider how you can integrate these skills into your daily work and decision-making processes.

For example, if you've practiced decision-making simulations related to project management, apply the techniques to your actual projects. Use the same analytical approach, consider multiple options, and reflect on the outcomes to continuously improve your decision-making skills.

By engaging in these simulations, you can develop a systematic approach to decision-making, improve your critical thinking abilities, and gain confidence in your judgment.

4. Role-Playing Adaptability

Adaptability is a crucial leadership trait that enables you to navigate through changes and uncertainties effectively. Role-playing exercises can help you practice and enhance your adaptability by simulating various challenging scenarios.

How You Can Do It:

Step 1: Select Relevant Scenarios

The first step in role-playing adaptability is to select scenarios that are relevant to your role and industry. These scenarios should reflect common challenges you might face, such as market shifts, internal crises, or unexpected changes in project scope. Begin by identifying key areas where adaptability is essential.

For example, if you are a business leader, scenarios might include:

- Navigating a sudden market downturn.
- Integrating new technology.
- Managing a team through organizational restructuring.

If you are in customer service, scenarios could involve handling difficult customers, implementing new service protocols, or adapting to sudden increases in demand.

Choosing realistic and relevant scenarios ensures that the role-playing exercises are directly applicable to your professional context, making the practice more effective and meaningful.

Step 2: Partner with a Colleague or Mentor

Role-playing is most effective when done with a partner who can provide feedback and different perspectives. Partner with a colleague, mentor, or coach who understands your role and can simulate different characters or situations.

Explain the purpose of the exercise and outline the scenario you want to practice. Ensure your partner is clear on their role and the context of the situation. For example, if the scenario involves managing a sudden market shift, your partner might play the role of a concerned stakeholder or a team member looking for guidance.

Collaborating with a partner adds realism to the exercise and provides an opportunity for immediate feedback, which is crucial for improving your adaptability skills.

Step 3: Simulate the Scenario

Begin the role-playing exercise by simulating the chosen scenario. Engage fully in the exercise, treating it as if it were a real situation. This immersion helps you practice reacting and adapting in a realistic context.

During the simulation, focus on how you handle the unexpected changes and challenges. Pay attention to your emotional responses, decision-making processes, and communication style. For instance, if the scenario involves an internal crisis, observe how you manage stress, communicate with your team, and make quick decisions.

Encourage your partner to act authentically and introduce new elements or twists to the scenario. This unpredictability helps simulate real-life complexities and tests your ability to remain flexible and composed under pressure.

Step 4: Reflect on the Experience

After completing the role-playing exercise, take time to reflect on the experience. This reflection is essential for identifying strengths and areas for improvement in your adaptability.

Consider the following questions during your reflection:
- *How did you feel during the simulation?*
- *What strategies did you use to adapt to the changes?*

- *Were there moments when you struggled to adapt? If so, why?*
- *What did you learn about your adaptability skills?*

For example, you might realize that you became anxious during a sudden market shift scenario, affecting your decision-making. Reflecting on this response helps you understand the triggers for your anxiety and explore strategies to manage it better in the future.

Step 5: Incorporate Feedback

Discuss the role-playing exercise with your partner and seek their feedback. Their observations can provide valuable insights into how you handled the scenario and areas where you can improve.

Ask your partner to share their perspective on your adaptability.

- *Did they notice any hesitation or uncertainty?*
- *Were there moments when you handled the situation particularly well?*
- *What suggestions do they have for enhancing your adaptability?*

For example, your partner might suggest that you improve your communication during crises by providing more frequent updates to your team. Incorporating this feedback helps you develop more effective strategies for managing similar situations in the future.

Step 6: Practice Different Scenarios

Adaptability involves being prepared for a wide range of situations. Practice different scenarios to build a diverse skill set and enhance your flexibility.

Choose a variety of scenarios that cover different aspects of your role and industry. This might include handling customer complaints, adapting to new technology, managing team conflicts, or navigating regulatory changes. Each scenario provides an opportunity to practice and refine different adaptability skills.

For instance, if you are a project manager, practice scenarios such as a key team member suddenly leaving the project, a major client changing their requirements, or encountering unexpected technical challenges. These varied scenarios ensure you are prepared for multiple types of changes and challenges.

Step 7: Develop Adaptability Strategies

Through repeated practice and reflection, identify and develop specific strategies that enhance your adaptability. These strategies can be tailored to your personal style and professional context.

Consider techniques such as mindfulness to stay calm under pressure, creative problem-solving to generate innovative solutions, and flexible planning to adjust strategies quickly. Document these strategies and incorporate them into your daily practice.

For example, you might develop a strategy of holding brief daily stand-up meetings with your team to quickly address any changes or challenges that arise. This approach ensures that everyone stays informed and can adapt collectively to new situations.

These exercises allow you to experiment with different approaches and responses in a safe environment, fostering flexibility and creative problem-solving skills.

6. Integrity Reflection

Integrity is a cornerstone of effective leadership, involving honesty, ethical behavior, and consistency in actions. Reflecting on your integrity helps you align your decisions and behaviors with your core values, fostering trust and respect within your team. Integrity reflection involves examining past decisions and actions to ensure they are in harmony with your ethical principles and values.

How You Can Do It:

Step 1: Identify Key Decisions and Actions

The first step in integrity reflection is to identify key decisions and actions in your career that had significant ethical implications. These decisions might include how you handled conflicts, managed resources, or dealt with challenging situations.

Start by listing important decisions you've made in the past few months or years. Focus on those that involved ethical considerations or had a substantial impact on others. For instance, decisions about hiring practices, resource allocation, or handling sensitive information are often ripe for reflection.

Once you have a list, choose one or two decisions to reflect on in-depth. This focused approach allows you to thoroughly examine each situation and gain valuable insights into your ethical decision-making process.

Step 2: Reflect on Motivations and Outcomes

Reflect on the motivations behind your decisions and the outcomes they produced. Understanding why you made a particular decision and the consequences it had is crucial for evaluating whether it aligned with your integrity and values.

Ask yourself questions such as:

- *What were the main factors influencing my decision?*
- *Were there any pressures or biases that affected my judgment?*
- *What were the short-term and long-term outcomes of my decision?*
- *Did the decision align with my core values and ethical principles?*

For example, if you made a decision to cut costs by reducing staff, consider whether the decision was driven solely by financial pressures or if it also considered the well-being of the employees affected. Reflect on the impact of this decision on team morale and the overall health of the organization.

Step 3: Assess Alignment with Core Values

Evaluate how well your decisions and actions align with your core values. This step involves comparing your behavior to the ethical standards and principles you strive to uphold.

Create a list of your core values, such as honesty, fairness, transparency, respect, and responsibility. For each decision or action, assess whether it upheld these values. Identify any discrepancies between your intended values and your actual behavior.

For instance, if transparency is one of your core values, consider whether you communicated openly and honestly with your team during a difficult decision. If there were gaps, reflect on why they occurred and how you can address them in the future.

Step 4: Learn from Ethical Challenges

Reflecting on ethical challenges and dilemmas you've faced can provide valuable learning opportunities. These situations often reveal the complexities of maintaining integrity and offer insights into how you can improve your ethical decision-making.

Identify specific ethical challenges you have encountered and analyze how you navigated them.

Consider the following questions:

- What made this situation ethically challenging?
- How did I approach the dilemma, and what factors did I consider?
- What were the ethical principles involved, and how did I prioritize them?
- What lessons did I learn from this experience?

For example, if you faced a conflict of interest situation, reflect on how you managed it and what steps you took to ensure fairness and transparency. Consider whether there were alternative actions you could have taken and how you can apply these lessons to future scenarios.

Step 5: Develop a Personal Code of Ethics

Creating a personal code of ethics can serve as a guide for maintaining integrity in your professional life. This code should outline the ethical standards and principles you commit to upholding in your decisions and actions.

To develop your personal code of ethics, start by identifying the core values that are most important to you. Write down specific behaviors and actions that exemplify these values. For example, if honesty is a core value, include statements like ***"I will communicate openly and truthfully, even when it is difficult."***

Include guidelines for handling common ethical dilemmas in your field. For instance, if you frequently deal with confidential information, outline steps for ensuring privacy and protecting sensitive data.

Review and update your personal code of ethics regularly to reflect any changes in your values or professional context. This living document helps you stay aligned with your integrity and provides a clear framework for ethical decision-making.

Step 6: Apply Integrity Reflection to Daily Practice

Integrating integrity reflection into your daily practice ensures that ethical considerations remain at the forefront of your decision-making. Regularly reflecting on your actions and decisions helps you stay committed to your values and continuously improve your ethical behavior.

Set aside time each week or month to reflect on recent decisions and actions. Use your personal code of ethics as a reference point and evaluate how well you are upholding your values. This regular practice helps reinforce your commitment to integrity and provides ongoing opportunities for growth.

For example, during your weekly reflection, review key decisions you made and assess whether they aligned with your core values. If you identify any discrepancies, consider how you can address them and improve your ethical decision-making in the future.

Integrity reflection is a powerful exercise for aligning your actions and decisions with your core values. Embrace this reflective practice to enhance your ethical leadership and foster a positive and principled work environment.

Inspiring and Motivating Others

Inspiring and motivating your team is crucial for driving high performance and achieving organizational goals. Effective leaders create an environment where team members feel valued, engaged, and motivated to contribute their best efforts.

Inspiring your team involves more than just setting goals and expectations. It requires creating an environment where team members feel motivated, valued, and empowered to perform their best.

Here are several techniques you can use to inspire your team:

1. Lead by Example

Leading by example is one of the most effective ways to inspire and motivate your team. When leaders model the behaviors, attitudes, and work ethic they expect from their team members, they set a powerful standard for others to follow. This approach not only fosters respect and trust but also creates a culture of accountability and high performance.

Activity: Model the Way

This activity involves consciously demonstrating the behaviors and attitudes you want to see in your team. By embodying these qualities in your daily interactions and work, you can effectively influence and inspire your team members to follow suit.

Here's how you can implement this activity:

Step 1: Identify Key Behaviors and Attitudes

Make a list of the key behaviors and attitudes that are crucial for your team's success. Reflect on the core values of your organization and how these behaviors align with those values. For example, if collaboration is a key value, you might list behaviors such as active listening, open communication, and willingness to help others.

You need to ensure that these behaviors are specific and actionable. For instance, instead of simply stating ***"be professional,"*** define what professionalism looks like in your context—timely responses to emails, punctuality in meetings, and respectful communication. By clearly defining these behaviors, you provide a concrete framework for what is expected.

Step 2: Demonstrate Consistently

Once you have identified the key behaviors and attitudes, commit to demonstrating them consistently. Consistency is critical because it shows that these behaviors are not just occasional efforts but are ingrained in the team's culture.

For example, if one of the behaviors is ***"active listening,"*** ensure that you practice it in every meeting. Show genuine interest in your team members' input, avoid interrupting, and provide thoughtful responses. Similarly, if ***"open communication"*** is a valued behavior, make it a habit to share information transparently and encourage feedback regularly.

Your actions speak louder than words. By consistently embodying these behaviors, you set a standard for your team and reinforce the importance of these values in everyday operations.

Step 3: Be Transparent and Honest

Transparency and honesty are fundamental to building trust and credibility with your team. Share your successes and challenges openly with your team. When you make a mistake, acknowledge it and discuss what you learned from the experience. This openness not only humanizes you as a leader but also encourages your team to be honest and transparent.

For instance, if a project does not go as planned, instead of assigning blame, discuss what went wrong, what can be improved, and how the team can move forward. This approach fosters a learning environment where team members feel safe to take risks and innovate.

Step 4: Engage in Regular Self-Reflection

Regular self-reflection helps you stay aligned with the behaviors and attitudes you want to model. Take time to evaluate your actions and identify areas where you can improve. This continuous improvement mindset not only benefits your leadership development but also sets an example for your team to follow.

Keep a journal where you document your daily interactions and reflect on how well you demonstrated the key behaviors.

Ask yourself questions like:

- *Did I actively listen in today's meeting?*
- *Was I open and transparent in my communications?*
- *What can I do better tomorrow?*

This practice keeps you accountable and focused on leading by example.

Step 5: Seek Feedback

Encourage your team to provide feedback on your leadership and the behaviors you are modeling. This feedback can offer valuable insights into how your actions are perceived and where you might need to adjust.

Create a safe space where team members feel comfortable sharing their thoughts. You can do this through anonymous surveys, one-on-one meetings, or open discussions.

For example, ask questions like:

- *How can I support you better?*
- *Are there areas where you feel I can improve?*
- *What behaviors have you noticed that positively impact our team?*

Listening to your team's feedback shows that you value their opinions and are committed to continuous improvement. It also reinforces the culture of open communication and mutual respect.

Step 6: Celebrate and Recognize Aligned Behaviors

When you see team members demonstrating the key behaviors and attitudes, recognize and celebrate their efforts. This positive reinforcement not only acknowledges their contributions but also reinforces the importance of these behaviors within the team.

For example, if a team member goes above and beyond to help a colleague, acknowledge their effort in a team meeting or through a personalized note. Highlighting these positive actions publicly encourages others to follow suit and fosters a supportive team environment.

This approach fosters a culture of accountability, trust, and high performance. Embrace this activity as an ongoing practice to continuously improve your leadership and positively impact your team's success.

2. Provide Autonomy and Empowerment

Being empowered is not just limited to you as a leader; it is crucial to extend this empowerment to your team members. Providing autonomy and empowerment involves giving your team the freedom to make decisions, take initiative, and own their responsibilities. This approach fosters a sense of ownership, boosts motivation, and enhances creativity, leading to higher performance and job satisfaction.

Activity: Delegate Meaningful Tasks

Delegating meaningful tasks is a practical way to provide autonomy and empowerment to your team. By assigning significant responsibilities, you show trust in your team's abilities and encourage them to take ownership of their work.

Here's how you can implement this activity:

Step 1: Identify Suitable Tasks

Begin by identifying tasks or projects that are meaningful and align with the team members' skills and interests. These tasks should be significant enough to challenge them and provide opportunities for growth. Avoid delegating only routine or menial tasks; instead, choose responsibilities that require critical thinking, creativity, and decision-making.

For instance, if you are leading a marketing team, you might delegate the responsibility of developing a new marketing campaign to a team member who has shown interest and aptitude in creative projects. Ensure that the task is well-defined, with clear objectives and expected outcomes.

Step 2: Provide Clear Guidelines and Objectives

Once you have identified the tasks, provide clear guidelines and objectives to ensure that the team members understand what is expected of them. This clarity helps them stay focused and aligned with the overall goals of the project or task.

Communicate the task's purpose, key deliverables, deadlines, and any specific requirements. For example, if you are delegating the creation of a marketing strategy, outline the target audience, budget constraints, and key performance indicators (KPIs) that will measure success. Providing this information upfront helps team members understand the scope and importance of the task.

Step 3: Offer Support and Resources

Empowerment does not mean abandoning your team members once a task is delegated. Offer the necessary support and resources to help them succeed. This support can include access to tools, training, and additional team members if needed.

Let your team know that you are available for guidance and assistance, but avoid micromanaging. Encourage them to come to you with questions or for advice while also giving them the space to explore solutions on their own. This balance of support and autonomy fosters a supportive environment where team members feel confident in their abilities.

Step 4: Encourage Decision-Making

Encourage team members to make decisions related to the tasks they have been assigned. This practice helps build their confidence and decision-making skills. Trust them to handle the task independently and resist the urge to intervene unless absolutely necessary.

For example, if a team member is leading a project, allow them to make choices about the project's direction, resource allocation, and timeline adjustments. This empowerment enables them to take ownership of the project and develop their leadership capabilities.

Step 5: Provide Constructive Feedback

As the task progresses, provide regular feedback to help team members stay on track and improve their performance. Constructive feedback should highlight what they are doing well and areas where they can improve.

Schedule periodic check-ins to discuss their progress and any challenges they may be facing. Offer specific suggestions and encouragement to help them overcome obstacles. For instance, if a team member is managing a client project, provide feedback on their client's communication and project management skills. This ongoing feedback helps them refine their approach and achieve better outcomes.

Step 6: Recognize and Celebrate Achievements

Finally, recognize and celebrate the achievements of team members once they complete the tasks successfully. Acknowledge their hard work and the positive impact of their contributions. This recognition reinforces the value of their efforts and motivates them to continue taking initiative.

Publicly acknowledge their accomplishments during team meetings, in company newsletters, or through personalized notes. Celebrating their successes not only boosts their morale but also sets a positive example for the rest of the team, encouraging a culture of empowerment and recognition.

Empowering your team means trusting them to handle their tasks and make decisions without constant oversight. This trust builds confidence and encourages them to take proactive steps to achieve their goals. When team members feel empowered, they are more likely to innovate, solve problems efficiently, and contribute to the organization's success.

3. Offer Constructive Feedback

Offering constructive feedback is a crucial component of effective leadership. Constructive feedback helps team members understand their strengths and areas for improvement, fostering continuous personal and professional development. When delivered effectively, feedback can boost morale, enhance performance, and create a culture of open communication and growth.

Constructive feedback is specific, actionable, and delivered in a supportive manner. It focuses on behaviors and outcomes rather than personal attributes, making it easier for the recipient to understand and act upon. Regular feedback helps team members stay aligned with organizational goals, reinforces positive behaviors, and provides guidance for improvement.

Activity: Feedback Fridays

Feedback Fridays is a structured activity designed to provide regular, constructive feedback to your team. This approach ensures that feedback is given consistently and systematically, promoting a culture of continuous improvement and open communication.

Here's how you can implement Feedback Fridays:

Step 1: Establish a Regular Schedule

Consistency is key to the success of Feedback Fridays. Set aside a specific time each week dedicated to providing feedback to your team. Communicate this schedule clearly to all team members so they know when to expect these sessions.

For example, you might choose to hold Feedback Fridays every Friday morning from 9:00 AM to 11:00 AM. Ensure that this time is reserved exclusively for feedback sessions, free from other interruptions or meetings. This regular schedule helps integrate feedback into the team's routine, making it a natural part of their workweek.

Step 2: Prepare Constructive Feedback

Before each session:

1. Take time to prepare your feedback.
2. Reflect on the week's activities, individual performances, and team dynamics.
3. Identify specific behaviors, actions, and outcomes that you want to address.

Use the "Start, Stop, Continue" method to structure your feedback:

- **Start:** Identify new behaviors or practices the team members should adopt.
- **Stop:** Highlight behaviors or practices that are unproductive or harmful.
- **Continue:** Reinforce positive behaviors and practices that should be maintained.

For example, if a team member has improved their project management skills but needs to work on their time management, your feedback might look like this: ***"I've noticed you've taken great initiative in managing our recent project (Continue). I think it would be beneficial if you could start using time-blocking techniques to manage your tasks more effectively (Start). However, I've observed that you sometimes overcommit to too many tasks at once, which impacts your overall productivity (Stop)."***

Step 3: Create a Supportive Environment

Create a supportive and non-threatening environment for your feedback sessions. Choose a comfortable setting where team members feel safe and valued. Approach the conversation with empathy and a genuine desire to help them improve.

Begin each session by acknowledging the team member's efforts and contributions. This positive start sets a constructive tone and shows that you recognize their hard work. For example, you might start by saying, ***"I appreciate all the hard work you've put into this project. Your dedication has really made a difference."***

Step 4: Deliver Feedback Effectively

When delivering feedback, be clear, specific, and focused on observable behaviors. Avoid vague statements and personal criticisms. Use concrete examples to illustrate your points and ensure that the feedback is actionable.

For instance, instead of saying, ***"You need to be more organized,"*** you could say, ***"I've noticed that your reports are often submitted late, which affects our project timelines. Let's discuss some strategies to help you stay on track with deadlines."***

Encourage a two-way dialogue during the feedback session. Allow the team member to share their perspective, ask questions, and discuss potential solutions. This collaborative approach fosters mutual understanding and commitment to improvement.

Step 5: Develop an Action Plan

Work with the team members to develop an action plan based on the feedback. This plan should outline specific steps they can take to address areas of improvement and build on their strengths. Set clear, achievable goals and establish a timeline for progress.

For example, if the feedback involves improving presentation skills, the action plan might include:

- Attending a public speaking workshop.
- Practicing presentations with a peer.
- Seeking opportunities to present at team meetings.

Review the action plan regularly and adjust it as needed. Provide ongoing support and resources to help the team member achieve their goals.

Step 6: Follow Up and Reinforce

Follow up on the feedback and action plan during subsequent Feedback Fridays. Discuss the progress made, any challenges faced, and the next steps. Reinforce positive changes and provide additional guidance as needed.

Celebrate successes and improvements, no matter how small. Recognizing progress boosts morale and motivates team members to continue working on their development. For instance, if a team member successfully improves their time management, acknowledge this achievement and discuss how it has positively impacted their performance.

By implementing Feedback Fridays, you can provide regular, structured feedback that helps your team members grow and succeed.

4. Foster a Collaborative Environment

Fostering a collaborative environment is essential for enhancing teamwork, creativity, and problem-solving within your organization. Collaboration encourages the sharing of diverse ideas and perspectives, leading to innovative solutions and improved performance. A collaborative environment also builds strong relationships among team members, increasing trust and morale.

Activity: Team-Building Projects

Team-building projects are a practical and engaging way to foster collaboration among team members. These projects can range from work-related tasks to fun activities designed to build trust and camaraderie. Here's how you can implement team-building projects:

Step 1: Identify Team-Building Objectives

Begin by identifying the specific objectives you want to achieve through team-building projects. These objectives could include improving communication, enhancing problem-solving skills, building trust, or fostering creativity.

For example, if your goal is to improve communication within the team, you might choose projects that require clear and effective information exchange. If building trust is the objective, consider activities that involve mutual support and cooperation.

Step 2: Select Appropriate Projects

Choose team-building projects that align with your objectives and are suitable for your team's interests and dynamics. The projects should be challenging enough to engage team members but not so difficult that they become frustrating.

Here are a few examples of team-building projects:

- **Work-Related Projects:** Assign a cross-functional team to tackle a specific business challenge, such as developing a new marketing strategy or improving a process. These projects provide opportunities for team members to collaborate on real work tasks.
- **Creative Workshops:** Organize workshops where team members can collaborate on creative tasks, such as brainstorming sessions, design thinking exercises, or innovation challenges. These activities stimulate creativity and encourage diverse perspectives.

- **Fun Activities:** Plan fun activities that promote teamwork and build relationships. Examples include escape rooms, scavenger hunts, cooking classes, and team sports. These activities provide a relaxed environment for team members to bond and develop trust.

Step 3: Set Clear Goals and Roles

For each team-building project, set clear goals and define the roles and responsibilities of each team member. This clarity ensures that everyone understands their contribution and how it fits into the larger objective.

Communicate the project's purpose, expected outcomes, and any specific guidelines or constraints. Assign roles based on team members' strengths and interests, ensuring that everyone has an opportunity to contribute meaningfully.

For example, in a project to develop a new marketing strategy, one team member might be responsible for market research, another for creative development, and another for budgeting and planning. Clearly defined roles help streamline collaboration and accountability.

Step 4: Facilitate Open Communication

Encourage open communication throughout the team-building project. Create an environment where team members feel comfortable sharing their ideas, asking questions, and providing feedback.

Use collaborative tools and platforms to facilitate communication, especially if your team is remote or distributed. Tools like Slack, Microsoft Teams, or Asana can help keep everyone connected and informed.

Regular check-ins and progress meetings can also help maintain open communication. Use these meetings to discuss updates, address any challenges, and celebrate milestones. For example, schedule weekly meetings to review progress and ensure everyone is on track.

Step 5: Encourage Mutual Support and Collaboration

Promote a culture of mutual support and collaboration by encouraging team members to help each other and work together towards common goals. Recognize and reward collaborative behaviors that contribute to the team's success.

Create opportunities for team members to collaborate on specific tasks or challenges. For example, pair team members with complementary skills to work on a complex problem or project. This approach fosters learning and skill-sharing, enhancing overall team performance.

Encourage a mindset of collective responsibility, where success is seen as a shared achievement. Celebrate team successes and acknowledge the contributions of each member, reinforcing the importance of collaboration.

Step 6: Reflect and Learn

After completing the team-building project, take time to reflect on the experience and gather feedback from team members. Discuss what went well, what challenges were encountered, and what could be improved in future projects.

Hold a debriefing session where team members can share their insights and reflections. Use this feedback to improve future team-building initiatives and enhance the collaborative culture within your team.

For example, after a creative workshop, ask team members to share their thoughts on the process, the outcomes, and any suggestions for improvement. This reflection helps identify best practices and areas for growth, ensuring continuous improvement in collaboration.

Creating a culture of collaboration involves promoting open communication, encouraging team members to work together on projects, and providing opportunities for joint problem-solving. By fostering collaboration, you can leverage the collective strengths of your team to achieve common goals more effectively.

5. Personalize Your Approach

Personalizing your approach to leadership involves understanding and catering to the individual needs, preferences, and motivations of your team members. This tailored approach helps build stronger relationships, enhances engagement, and improves overall performance. When team members feel seen and valued as individuals, they are more likely to be motivated, committed, and satisfied with their work.

Activity: One-on-One Meetings

One-on-one meetings are a powerful tool for personalizing your approach to leadership. These meetings provide a dedicated time for you to connect with each team member, understand their needs, and offer tailored support and guidance. Here's how you can implement one-on-one meetings effectively:

Step 1: Schedule Regular Meetings

Consistency is crucial for effective one-on-one meetings. Schedule regular meetings with each team member, ideally on a weekly or bi-weekly basis. Communicate the schedule in advance and ensure that these meetings are a priority for both you and your team members.

For example, you might schedule one-on-one meetings every Tuesday morning, allocating 30 minutes to an hour for each team member. Consistent scheduling demonstrates your commitment to their development and provides a reliable forum for ongoing dialogue.

Step 2: Prepare for Each Meeting

Preparation is key to making the most of one-on-one meetings. Before each meeting, review your notes from previous discussions and identify any follow-up items. Consider the team member's current projects, challenges, and achievements.

Prepare a list of topics to discuss, but also be open to addressing any concerns or questions they may have. This preparation helps ensure that the meeting is focused, productive, and relevant to the team member's needs.

For instance, if a team member is working on a major project, review their progress and think about any specific feedback or support they might need. Preparing thoughtful questions and discussion points shows that you value their time and contributions.

Step 3: Create a Safe and Supportive Environment

One-on-one meetings should take place in a comfortable and private setting where team members feel safe to speak openly. This environment encourages candid conversations and helps build trust.

Begin each meeting with a friendly and supportive tone. Show genuine interest in their well-being by asking about their recent experiences, challenges, and successes. Listen actively and empathetically, allowing them to express their thoughts and feelings without interruption.

For example, start the meeting with a simple question, ***"How have things been going for you this week?"*** This open-ended question invites them to share both personal and professional updates, fostering a more holistic understanding of their situation.

Step 4: Tailor Your Support and Guidance

Use the insights gained from your discussions to provide personalized support and guidance. Tailor your feedback and advice to address their specific needs, goals, and challenges.

For example, if a team member expresses difficulty managing their workload, work together to develop time management strategies or adjust their responsibilities. If they are seeking professional development opportunities, help them identify relevant training programs or projects that align with their interests.

Personalized support might also involve recognizing and leveraging their unique strengths. For instance, if a team member excels at creative thinking, find opportunities for them to contribute to brainstorming sessions or innovative projects.

Step 5: Set Clear Goals and Follow Up

Collaboratively set clear, achievable goals for their development and progress. These goals should be specific, measurable, and aligned with their career aspirations and the team's objectives.

During the meeting, discuss potential goals and create an action plan with concrete steps and timelines. For example, if a team member wants to improve their presentation skills, set a goal to deliver a presentation at the next team meeting and identify steps for preparation and practice.

Regularly follow up on these goals in subsequent meetings. Review their progress, celebrate achievements, and adjust the action plan as needed. This follow-up shows that you are invested in their growth and helps them stay accountable and motivated.

Step 6: Encourage Feedback and Two-Way Communication

One-on-one meetings are also an opportunity for you to receive feedback from your team members. Encourage open and honest communication about your leadership and any areas where you can improve.

Ask for their input on how you can better support them and create a more effective team environment. This feedback loop fosters mutual respect and continuous improvement.

For example, you might ask, ***"Is there anything I can do differently to help you succeed?" or "How can I improve my support for our team?"*** Actively listening to their feedback and taking action on their suggestions demonstrates your commitment to being an effective and responsive leader.

Step 7: Document and Reflect

Document key points and action items from each one-on-one meeting. Keeping detailed notes helps you track progress, follow up on commitments, and ensure continuity in your discussions.

Reflect on the outcomes of your one-on-one meetings and your overall approach to personalized leadership. Consider what's working well and where you can make adjustments to better support your team.

Personalizing your approach requires active listening, empathy, and a genuine interest in your team members' professional and personal growth. It involves recognizing their unique strengths and challenges and providing support and opportunities that align with their goals and aspirations.

By implementing these techniques, you can create an environment where your team feels motivated, valued, and empowered. This approach not only enhances individual performance but also drives collective success and fosters a positive, collaborative workplace culture.

Recognizing and Celebrating Achievements

Knowing how to effectively recognize and celebrate your team's achievements is essential for maintaining high morale and motivation. Celebrations and recognition acknowledge the hard work and dedication of your team members, reinforcing positive behaviors and encouraging continued excellence. By publicly and personally appreciating their efforts, you create a culture of recognition that drives engagement and productivity.

Here are several ways to recognize and celebrate achievements:

1. Public Recognition

Public recognition involves acknowledging and celebrating the achievements of your team members in a visible and formal manner. This type of recognition not only boosts individual morale but also sets a positive example for the entire team, reinforcing desired behaviors and encouraging others to strive for similar accomplishments. Public recognition can take various forms, including announcements during meetings, highlighting achievements in company newsletters, or sharing successes on social media platforms.

Benefits of Public Recognition:

- **Boosts Morale:** Public acknowledgment of achievements makes team members feel valued and appreciated, enhancing their motivation and job satisfaction.
- **Encourages Positive Behavior:** Highlighting specific actions and achievements publicly reinforces the behaviors you want to see more of in your team.
- **Fosters a Positive Culture:** Regular public recognition contributes to a supportive and appreciative work environment, strengthening team cohesion and engagement.
- **Increases Visibility:** Recognizing achievements in public forums can increase the visibility of individual contributions, which can be particularly motivating for high performers.

Public recognition not only boosts individual morale but also cultivates a supportive and motivating team culture. This approach helps reinforce positive behaviors and drives overall team success.

Activity: Recognition Board

A Recognition Board is a practical and engaging way to implement public recognition within your team or organization. It serves as a central place where achievements, big and small, can be highlighted and celebrated. This can be a physical board in a common area or a digital platform accessible to all team members.

How to Implement a Recognition Board:

Step 1: Choose a Format

Decide whether you want to create a physical or digital Recognition Board. A physical board could be placed in a prominent location such as a break room, hallway, or office entrance. A digital board can be created using platforms like Slack, Microsoft Teams, Trello, or a dedicated section on your company intranet.

When choosing a format, consider the preferences and accessibility of your team. A physical board might be more impactful in an office environment where team members can see it daily, while a digital board might be more suitable for remote or distributed teams.

Step 2: Set Clear Guidelines

Establish clear guidelines for how and what to recognize on the board. Define the types of achievements that will be highlighted, such as project completions, outstanding teamwork, innovative ideas, or exceptional customer service.

For example, you might decide to recognize any accomplishment that goes above and beyond regular job duties or significantly contributes to team goals. Clarify who can post recognitions – whether it's open to all team members or managed by a designated person.

Step 3: Encourage Participation

Encourage team members to actively participate in using the Recognition Board. Foster a culture where recognizing and celebrating each other's successes becomes a regular practice.

Promote the board in team meetings and internal communications, explaining its purpose and how team members can contribute. Lead by example by regularly posting recognitions yourself, showing that you value and appreciate your team's efforts.

Step 4: Highlight Achievements Regularly

Make it a habit to update the Recognition Board regularly with new achievements. During team meetings, take a few minutes to review recent recognitions, providing a brief overview of the highlighted accomplishments and expressing your appreciation.

This regular update not only keeps the board dynamic and engaging but also reinforces the importance of recognizing and celebrating success.

Step 5: Make it Visually Appealing

Whether physical or digital, ensure that the Recognition Board is visually appealing and engaging. Use colors, images, and different formats to highlight achievements in an attractive way.

For a physical board, consider using different sections for various types of recognitions, such as **"Employee of the Month," "Team Achievements," and "Customer Kudos."** For a digital board, use tags, categories, or channels to organize the recognitions.

Use the Recognition Board to celebrate significant milestones and team achievements collectively. This could include completing major projects, reaching sales targets, or achieving company-wide goals.

2. Personalized Rewards

Personalized rewards are a highly effective way to recognize and appreciate the unique contributions of your team members. Unlike generic rewards, personalized rewards take into account the individual preferences, interests, and needs of each team member, making the recognition more meaningful and impactful. By tailoring rewards to what genuinely resonates with each person, you show that you value them as individuals and appreciate their specific efforts and achievements.

Benefits of Personalized Rewards:

- **Increases Motivation:** When rewards are personalized, team members feel that their hard work is genuinely acknowledged, which boosts their motivation and engagement.
- **Enhances Job Satisfaction:** Personalized rewards contribute to a higher sense of job satisfaction, as they reflect an understanding of individual preferences and needs.
- **Fosters Loyalty:** Showing that you care about your team members on a personal level can increase their loyalty to the organization, reducing turnover rates.
- **Encourages Positive Behavior:** Tailored rewards reinforce the behaviors and achievements you want to see more of in your team.

By implementing personalized rewards, you can create a more engaged and motivated workforce that feels valued and appreciated. This approach enhances the overall team dynamics and drives a culture of excellence.

Activity: Personalized Appreciation Notes

Personalized appreciation notes are a simple yet powerful way to recognize and thank your team members for their hard work and contributions.

Here's how you can effectively implement personalized appreciation notes:

Step 1: Identify Achievements

Start by identifying the specific achievements and contributions of your team members. Pay attention to their recent projects, challenges they have overcome, and any instances where they have gone above and beyond their regular duties.

For example, if a team member successfully led a critical project to completion or provided exceptional support during a busy period, make a note of these accomplishments. This ensures that your appreciation is specific and relevant.

Step 2: Personalize the Message

When writing the appreciation note, personalize it by addressing the team member by name and mentioning their specific achievements. Highlight the impact of their contributions on the team and the organization.

For instance, instead of writing a generic ***"Thank you for your hard work,"*** you could say, ***"Dear [Name], I want to personally thank you for your outstanding work on the XYZ project. Your dedication and innovative approach were key to its success, and we couldn't have achieved this milestone without your efforts."***

By personalizing the message, you demonstrate that you have taken the time to recognize their unique contributions, making the appreciation more meaningful.

Step 3: Be Genuine and Specific

Ensure that your note is genuine and heartfelt. Avoid generic phrases and focus on the specific actions and behaviors that you are acknowledging. Use a sincere tone to convey your appreciation.

For example, ***"Your commitment to meeting tight deadlines and your willingness to assist your colleagues during the recent product launch were truly commendable. Your hard work and positive attitude have made a significant difference, and I am grateful for your contributions."***

Genuine appreciation fosters a stronger connection and makes the recognition more impactful.

Step 4: Deliver the Note Personally

Whenever possible, deliver the appreciation note personally. Handing it over in person adds a personal touch and allows you to express your gratitude face-to-face. If in-person delivery is not feasible, consider delivering it through a handwritten note placed on their desk or mailed to their home.

For remote team members, a personalized email can also be effective, but ensure that it is well-crafted and sincere. The personal delivery of appreciation enhances the impact and shows that you value their contributions enough to make the extra effort.

After delivering the appreciation note, follow up with the team member to reinforce your gratitude and offer any additional support or feedback. This follow-up can be a brief conversation where you reiterate your appreciation and discuss any ongoing or future projects.

For example, during a follow-up conversation, you might say, ***"I hope you received my note. I just wanted to reiterate how much I appreciate your hard work on the XYZ project. Your efforts have set a high standard for our team, and I'm excited to see what you'll accomplish next."***

This follow-up reinforces the recognition and encourages ongoing dialogue and engagement.

Writing a thoughtful, personalized note shows that you have taken the time to acknowledge their specific achievements and appreciate their efforts.

3. Celebration Events

Celebration events are an integral part of recognizing and appreciating your team's hard work and achievements. These events go beyond formal recognition and create memorable experiences that foster team spirit and camaraderie.

Benefits of Celebration Events:

- **Strengthen Team Bonds:** Celebrations bring team members together in a relaxed and enjoyable setting, helping to build stronger interpersonal relationships.
- **Boost Morale:** Acknowledging and celebrating achievements makes team members feel valued and appreciated, which can significantly boost morale and motivation.
- **Encourage a Positive Culture:** Regular celebration of achievements fosters a culture of recognition and appreciation, which can lead to higher levels of engagement and productivity.
- Enhance Job Satisfaction: Celebrations provide a break from routine work, allowing team members to recharge and return to their tasks with renewed energy and enthusiasm.

By organizing celebration events, you create a positive and supportive work environment where achievements are acknowledged and valued.

Activity: Achievement Celebrations

Achievement celebrations are structured events designed to recognize and celebrate the milestones and successes of your team. These celebrations can be tailored to fit the nature of the achievement and the preferences of your team.

Here's how you can implement effective achievement celebrations:

Step 1: Identify Milestones and Achievements

Start by identifying the milestones and achievements that warrant celebration. These could include the completion of major projects, reaching significant sales targets, anniversaries with the company, or exceptional individual or team performances.

For example, if your team has successfully launched a new product or met a challenging deadline, these are perfect opportunities for celebration. Keep a list of notable achievements to ensure that no accomplishment goes unrecognized.

Step 2: Plan the Celebration

Plan the celebration event based on the nature of the achievement and the preferences of your team. Consider the size of the team, the significance of the achievement, and the available budget.

Celebrations can take various forms:

- **Informal Gatherings:** These can include team lunches, after-work outings, or coffee breaks where the team can relax and socialize. For example, you might take the team out for a celebratory lunch after completing a major project.
- **Formal Events:** These can include award ceremonies, company parties, or team-building retreats. For a more significant milestone, you might organize an award ceremony to present certificates or trophies to the team members involved.
- **Virtual Celebrations:** For remote teams, consider virtual celebrations such as online parties, virtual happy hours, or recognition during video meetings. Use tools like Zoom or Microsoft Teams to bring the team together in a virtual space.

Step 3: Personalize the Celebration

Personalize the celebration to make it meaningful for the team members involved. Consider their preferences and interests when planning the event. For instance, if your team enjoys outdoor activities, you might plan a picnic or a hiking trip.

Include personalized elements such as thank-you speeches, individual recognitions, or customized awards. For example, during the celebration, you could give a short speech highlighting the specific contributions of each team member and how their efforts led to the achievement.

Step 4: Communicate and Involve the Team

Communicate the details of the celebration to the team well in advance. Ensure that everyone is aware of the date, time, and location of the event. Involve the team in the planning process by seeking their input on the type of celebration they would enjoy.

For example, send out a survey or have a brainstorming session to gather ideas for the celebration. This involvement ensures that the event reflects the team's preferences and increases their excitement and participation.

Step 5: Create a Memorable Experience

Focus on creating a memorable and enjoyable experience for the team. This can include thoughtful touches such as personalized awards, special decorations, or themed activities that make the event unique.

For instance, if celebrating a project completion, you might decorate the venue with project-related themes or create a slideshow highlighting key moments and contributions. Provide opportunities for team members to share their experiences and stories related to the achievement.

Step 6: Reflect and Appreciate

During the celebration, take time to reflect on the journey and appreciate the efforts that led to the achievement. Acknowledge the challenges overcome, the teamwork displayed, and the dedication shown by the team members.

Give a speech or presentation that highlights the significance of the achievement and expresses genuine gratitude for everyone's contributions. Encourage team members to share their thoughts and feelings about the accomplishment and the celebration.

After the celebration, follow up with the team to gather feedback and assess the impact of the event. Use this feedback to improve future celebrations and ensure that they continue to resonate with the team.

Celebration events can range from informal gatherings, such as team lunches or after-work outings, to formal award ceremonies. These events provide an opportunity to publicly acknowledge accomplishments, build stronger relationships, and boost overall morale.

4. Peer Recognition Programs
Peer recognition programs are an effective way to foster a culture of appreciation and support within your team.

Benefits of Peer Recognition Programs:

- **Builds a Supportive Culture:** Encourages a collaborative and supportive work environment where team members actively appreciate each other's efforts.
- **Increases Engagement:** Peer recognition can boost morale and engagement, as employees feel valued and acknowledged by their peers.
- **Enhances Team Cohesion:** Promotes a sense of belonging and strengthens relationships among team members.
- **Encourages Positive Behavior:** Reinforces positive behaviors and achievements, motivating others to strive for similar recognition.

Activity: Peer-to-Peer Recognition
Peer-to-peer recognition is a structured activity where team members can nominate and celebrate each other's achievements. This program can be implemented in various ways, such as through regular nominations, a recognition board, or during team meetings.

Here's how you can implement an effective peer-to-peer recognition program:
Step 1: Establish a Framework

Create a clear framework for your peer-to-peer recognition program. Define the criteria for recognition, the process for nominating peers, and how recognitions will be communicated and celebrated.

For example, you might decide to recognize behaviors such as teamwork, innovation, exceptional customer service, or going above and beyond in their roles. Ensure the criteria are well-defined and communicated to all team members.

Step 2: Choose a Platform

Decide on the platform for your peer-to-peer recognition program. This could be a physical recognition board, a dedicated channel in a collaboration tool like Slack or Microsoft Teams, or an online form where team members can submit nominations.

If you choose a digital platform, ensure it is easily accessible and user-friendly. For a physical board, place it in a common area where all team members can see and contribute to it regularly.

Step 3: Encourage Participation

Promote the peer-to-peer recognition program and encourage active participation. Explain the purpose and benefits of the program during team meetings and through internal communications.

Lead by example by nominating peers yourself and highlighting the importance of recognizing each other's efforts. Encourage team members to take part by sharing stories of impactful recognitions and how they positively influenced the team.

Step 4: Facilitate Regular Nominations

Set a regular schedule for nominations to keep the recognition consistent and ongoing. This could be weekly, bi-weekly, or monthly, depending on your team's dynamics and workload.

For example, you might have a **"Recognition Friday"** where team members can submit nominations throughout the week, and the recognitions are shared during a

Friday team meeting. Provide a simple and straightforward process for submitting nominations to make it easy for everyone to participate.

Step 5: Highlight and Celebrate Recognitions

Create opportunities to publicly celebrate and highlight the recognitions. This can be done during team meetings, in newsletters, or on the recognition board.

During team meetings, set aside time to read out the nominations and celebrate the recognized individuals. For digital platforms, regularly post the recognitions in the dedicated channel and encourage team members to add their congratulations and comments.

For example, during a team meeting, you might say, ***"I'd like to take a moment to recognize [Name] for their outstanding teamwork and support during the recent project. [Name] was nominated by [Peer's Name], who highlighted their willingness to help and their positive attitude. Thank you, [Name], for embodying our team values."***

Step 6: Provide Tangible Rewards

Consider pairing peer recognitions with tangible rewards to add an extra layer of appreciation. These rewards could include small gifts, certificates, or special privileges like a preferred parking spot or an extra day off.

Ensure the rewards are meaningful and relevant to your team members. Personalize the rewards when possible to show that you've considered the preferences and contributions of the recognized individual.

Step 7: Gather Feedback and Improve

Regularly gather feedback from your team about the peer-to-peer recognition program to understand what's working well and what can be improved. Use this feedback to refine the program and keep it effective and engaging.

Send out periodic surveys or hold feedback sessions where team members can share their thoughts and suggestions. For example, you might ask, ***"How do you feel about*** *the current peer recognition process? What changes would make it more effective and enjoyable for you?"*

Peer recognition programs are a powerful way to build a supportive and appreciative team culture. By implementing a structured peer-to-peer recognition activity, you can enhance team cohesion, boost morale, and reinforce positive behaviors. Embrace this approach to create an environment where team members feel valued and motivated by their peers, driving collective success and satisfaction.

These programs empower team members to recognize and celebrate each other's contributions, enhancing mutual respect and camaraderie.

Persuasion and Influence

Persuasion and influence are critical skills for any leader or entrepreneur. The ability to effectively persuade others can lead to successful negotiations, stronger partnerships, and more effective team leadership. Building trust and credibility is fundamental to influencing others, as it ensures that people believe in and support your vision and decisions.

Strategies for Persuading Others in Business

Persuading others in business requires a combination of communication skills, emotional intelligence, and strategic thinking.

Here are some key strategies to enhance your persuasive abilities:

1. Understand Your Audience

Understanding your audience is the cornerstone of effective persuasion. It involves gaining insights into their needs, values, preferences, and concerns.

Here's how you can deepen your understanding of your audience:

Step 1: Conduct Research

Before engaging with your audience, gather as much information as possible about them. This can include their professional background, interests, challenges, and goals. Use various sources such as social media profiles, company websites, industry reports, and personal interactions to build a comprehensive profile.

For example, if you are preparing for a presentation to a potential client, research their company's history, mission, and recent achievements. Understand the client's industry trends and specific challenges they might be facing. This background knowledge allows you to tailor your pitch to address their unique needs and position your solution as the best fit.

You can find this information through several methods:

- **Online Research:** Use LinkedIn to view professional profiles and see career history and interests. Visit the company's website to understand their mission, values, and recent news. Read industry reports to stay informed about market trends and challenges.
- **Direct Interaction:** Engage in conversations with people who know your audience, such as colleagues, industry contacts, or mutual acquaintances. Attending industry events and networking can also provide valuable insights.
- **Surveys and Feedback:** If possible, conduct surveys or request feedback from your audience to understand their preferences and pain points directly.

When doing your research, make sure to verify the accuracy of the information from multiple sources. This thorough understanding helps you craft a message that resonates deeply with your audience.

Step 2: Identify Key Stakeholders

Identify the key stakeholders within your audience. These are the individuals who have the most influence over the decision-making process. Understanding their roles, responsibilities, and interests will help you tailor your message to address their specific needs and concerns.

For example, in a sales pitch, identify the decision-makers, such as the CEO, CFO, or department heads, and understand what each one values most. The CEO might prioritize the overall strategic fit of your solution, while the CFO might focus on cost-effectiveness and return on investment.

Step 3: Understand Their Motivations

Understanding the motivations of your audience is critical for effective persuasion. What drives them? What are their primary goals and objectives? Are they motivated by financial gains, career advancement, customer satisfaction, or innovation?

For instance, if you are pitching a new software solution to a tech-savvy audience, emphasize the innovative features and how it can streamline their operations. If your audience is more focused on cost savings, highlight the long-term financial benefits and the efficiency gains of your solution.

Step 4: Tailor Your Message

Once you have gathered comprehensive information about your audience, tailor your message to align with their needs and preferences. Use language, examples, and data that resonate with them. Highlight how your proposal addresses their specific challenges and supports their goals.

For example, if you are presenting to a board of directors concerned with regulatory compliance, focus on how your solution ensures compliance and mitigates risks. Use relevant data and case studies to support your claims.

Step 5: Engage and Listen

Engagement is not just about speaking; it also involves active listening. During your interaction, pay close attention to verbal and non-verbal cues. Understand their feedback, questions, and concerns. This real-time information can help you adjust your approach and respond effectively.

For instance, during a meeting, if a stakeholder raises a concern about the implementation timeline, address it directly by providing a detailed plan and examples of successful implementations. Listening and responding appropriately show that you value their input and are committed to meeting their needs.

When you tailor your message to resonate with your audience, you increase the likelihood of gaining their support and achieving your desired outcomes.

2. Build a Strong Case

Building a strong case is essential for persuading others in business. A well-structured and compelling argument provides the necessary support for your proposal and makes it more convincing to your audience.

Here's how you can build a strong case:

Step 1: Gather Relevant Data and Evidence

Start by collecting all the relevant data and evidence that support your proposal. This includes statistical data, case studies, expert opinions, and any other factual information that can substantiate your claims.

For example, if you are proposing a new marketing strategy, gather data on market trends, customer behavior, and previous campaign results. Include statistics that demonstrate the potential reach and impact of your strategy. Use case studies from similar successful campaigns to illustrate the effectiveness of your approach.

When gathering data, ensure that your sources are credible and reliable. Using reputable sources enhances the credibility of your case and makes it more convincing.

Step 2: Structure Your Argument Logically

Organize your argument in a clear and logical manner. A well-structured argument helps your audience follow your reasoning and understand the rationale behind your proposal. Start with a strong introduction that outlines the main points of your case. Then, present your evidence in a logical sequence, ensuring each point builds on the previous one.

For example, begin by stating the problem or opportunity, followed by an analysis of the current situation. Next, introduce your proposed solution and support it with relevant data and examples. Conclude with a summary that reinforces your main points and calls to action.

It is important to remember when structuring your argument to avoid overwhelming your audience with too much information. Focus on the most compelling evidence and present it in a concise and clear manner.

Step 3: Use Clear and Persuasive Language

The language you use can significantly impact the persuasiveness of your argument. Use clear, concise, and persuasive language to convey your message effectively. Avoid jargon and technical terms that may confuse your audience. Instead, use straightforward language that is easy to understand.

For example, instead of saying, ***"Our marketing strategy will leverage multi-channel integration to enhance customer engagement,"*** you could say, ***"Our marketing strategy will use multiple platforms to better connect with our customers."***

Use active voice and strong verbs to make your statements more impactful. For instance, ***"This strategy will increase sales by 20%,"*** is more powerful than, ***"Sales are expected to increase by 20% with this strategy."***

Step 4: Address Counterarguments

Anticipate potential objections and address them proactively in your argument. This shows that you have thoroughly considered different perspectives and strengthens your case by demonstrating that it can withstand scrutiny.

For example, if you anticipate that cost might be a concern for your proposed marketing strategy, address it by highlighting the long-term return on investment and cost savings from increased efficiency.

Acknowledge valid concerns and provide well-reasoned responses that reinforce the strength of your proposal. This approach not only builds credibility but also shows respect for your audience's viewpoints.

Step 5: Use Visual Aids

Visual aids such as charts, graphs, and slides can enhance your argument by making complex data more accessible and engaging. Visuals help illustrate key points and make your case more memorable.

For example, use a graph to show the projected growth in sales with your proposed strategy, or a pie chart to illustrate the market share of different competitors. Ensure that your visuals are clear, professional, and directly related to your key points.

Visual aids should complement your verbal presentation and not overwhelm it. Keep them simple and focused on highlighting the most important data.

Step 6: Practice Your Delivery

The way you present your case is just as important as the content itself. Practice your delivery to ensure that you can present your argument confidently and fluently. Pay attention to your tone, pace, and body language.

For example, maintain eye contact with your audience to build connection and trust. Use a confident tone and avoid filler words like "um" and "uh." Practice your presentation multiple times to become familiar with the material and to smooth out any rough spots.

Consider rehearsing in front of a colleague or friend to get feedback on your delivery and make any necessary adjustments.

By following these steps, you can create a compelling and persuasive argument that effectively convinces your audience and achieves your desired outcomes.

3. Use Emotional Appeals

While logical reasoning and solid evidence are crucial in building a persuasive case, emotional appeals can significantly enhance your ability to connect with your audience and drive them to action.

Here's how you can effectively use emotional appeals:

Step 1: Understand the Emotional Landscape

Start by understanding the emotional landscape of your audience. What are their hopes, fears, aspirations, and pain points? Knowing these emotional drivers allows you to tailor your message to resonate with their feelings and experiences.

For example, if your audience is concerned about environmental sustainability, highlighting the eco-friendly aspects of your proposal can evoke feelings of responsibility and urgency. Similarly, if your audience values innovation and progress, framing your message to highlight these elements can inspire excitement and engagement.

When understanding the emotional landscape, consider conducting surveys, interviews, or focus groups to gather direct insights from your audience. This approach helps you capture their emotional drivers accurately.

Step 2: Tell a Story

Stories are powerful tools for engaging emotions. They make abstract concepts concrete and relatable, allowing your audience to see themselves in the narrative. A well-told story can evoke empathy, excitement, or inspiration, making your message more impactful.

For instance, instead of just presenting data on the benefits of a new product, share a story about a customer who experienced a significant positive change due to the product. This personal touch can make your audience feel more connected to the idea and more likely to support it.

Ensure that your story is relevant and aligns with the message you want to convey. Keep it concise and focused, emphasizing the key emotional points that will resonate with your audience.

Step 3: Use Vivid Language

Vivid, descriptive language can evoke strong emotions and create a lasting impression. Instead of using technical jargon or bland terms, choose words that paint a picture and stir feelings.

For example, instead of saying, ***"Our solution is effective and efficient,"*** you could say, ***"Our solution is a game-changer that revolutionizes how we tackle challenges, bringing about unprecedented efficiency and effectiveness."*** The latter is more likely to inspire excitement and engagement.

Pay attention to the tone of your language as well. A positive, enthusiastic tone can evoke excitement, while a calm, reassuring tone can evoke trust and confidence.

Step 4: Appeal to Shared Values

Appealing to shared values can create a strong emotional connection with your audience. Identify the core values that you and your audience have in common and emphasize them in your message.

For instance, if your audience values community and collaboration, highlight how your proposal fosters teamwork and collective success. If they value integrity and transparency, emphasize these aspects in your approach.

By aligning your message with the values your audience holds dear, you can create a sense of unity and shared purpose, making your case more compelling.

Step 5: Create a Sense of Urgency

Creating a sense of urgency can motivate your audience to take immediate action. Highlighting the potential consequences of inaction or the benefits of timely action can evoke emotions such as fear of missing out or the excitement of seizing an opportunity.

For example, if you are proposing a time-sensitive project, emphasize the immediate benefits and the risks of delaying. Use phrases like, ***"Act now to secure these benefits,"*** or ***"Don't miss out on this unique opportunity."***

Ensure that the urgency is genuine and not exaggerated, as this can backfire and lead to distrust.

Step 6: Show Genuine Passion

Your passion and enthusiasm can be contagious. When you genuinely believe in what you are presenting, it shows, and it can inspire your audience to share your excitement and commitment.

Speak with energy and conviction, and use body language that conveys your enthusiasm. Share personal anecdotes or experiences that demonstrate your genuine belief in your proposal.

For example, if you are passionate about a new sustainability initiative, share why it matters to you personally and how you've seen its impact firsthand. This personal touch can make your message more relatable and inspiring.

Emotional appeals engage your audience on a deeper level, creating a sense of connection and urgency that purely logical arguments might lack. By tapping into emotions such as empathy, excitement, or concern, you can make your message more compelling and memorable.

4. Establish Common Ground

Establishing common ground is a crucial strategy in persuasion, as it helps build rapport and trust with your audience. When you identify and emphasize shared goals, values, or experiences, you create a sense of connection and mutual understanding. This approach makes your audience more receptive to your ideas and more likely to support your proposals.

Here's how you can effectively establish common ground:

Step 1: Identify Shared Goals and Interests

Start by identifying the goals and interests you share with your audience. These commonalities can serve as a foundation for building rapport and aligning your message with their priorities.

For example, if you are presenting a new project to a team of stakeholders, focus on how the project aligns with the organization's overall mission and objectives. Highlight the shared goal of achieving business growth, improving customer satisfaction, or enhancing operational efficiency.

Understanding shared goals and interests requires thorough research and active listening. Engage with your audience to learn about their priorities and concerns, and use this information to tailor your message.

Step 2: Highlight Common Experiences

Common experiences can create a strong sense of connection and understanding. By referencing experiences that you and your audience have in common, you can build empathy and demonstrate that you understand their perspective.

For instance, if you are addressing a team that has recently gone through significant changes, acknowledge these changes and relate them to your own experiences. You might say, *"We've all experienced the challenges of adapting to new systems, but this project will streamline our processes and make our work more efficient."*

Sharing stories or anecdotes that resonate with your audience's experiences can make your message more relatable and compelling.

Step 3: Use Inclusive Language

Using inclusive language helps create a sense of unity and collaboration. Words like *"we,"* *"us,"* and *"our"* emphasize collective effort and shared responsibility, making your audience feel like they are part of the solution.

For example, instead of saying, *"I believe this project will benefit the company,"* say, *"We can all benefit from the success of this project."* This subtle shift in language fosters a sense of teamwork and shared commitment to the goals being discussed.

Step 4: Address Concerns and Acknowledge Differences

While it's important to highlight commonalities, acknowledging differences and addressing concerns transparently is also crucial. This approach shows that you respect and understand diverse perspectives, which can strengthen trust and credibility.

For example, if you know that some stakeholders have reservations about your proposal, acknowledge these concerns and provide clear, evidence-based responses. You might say, *"I understand that some of you may be concerned about the initial costs, but let's look at the long-term benefits and ROI that this investment will bring."*

Step 5: Emphasize Mutual Benefits

Emphasizing mutual benefits reinforces the idea that your proposal is a win-win situation. Clearly articulate how your proposal will benefit all parties involved, addressing their specific needs and goals.

For instance, when proposing a partnership, highlight how each party stands to gain from the collaboration. ***"This partnership will allow us to leverage each other's strengths, driving innovation and expanding our market reach for mutual growth."***

By fostering a sense of unity and understanding, you can create a more receptive and collaborative environment for your proposals. This approach not only enhances your persuasive efforts but also builds stronger, more trusting relationships with your audience.

5. Address Objections Proactively

There will be times when your audience has concerns or objections about your proposal. Addressing these objections proactively is crucial for maintaining credibility and demonstrating that you have thoroughly considered all aspects of your proposal. By anticipating and addressing potential objections, you can build trust and make your case more compelling.

Here is how you can address objections proactively:

Step 1: Anticipate Objections

Before presenting your proposal, think about the possible objections your audience might have. Some objections will include concerns about costs, risks, feasibility, or the potential impact on current operations. List these potential objections and prepare thoughtful responses for each one.

For example, if you are proposing a new software implementation, anticipate objections such as:

- *What will be the initial cost?*
- *How will it affect our current workflows*
- *What are the potential risks involved?*

Step 2: Gather Supporting Evidence

Prepare evidence to support your responses to anticipated objections. This evidence can include data, case studies, expert opinions, or examples of similar successful implementations.

For instance, if cost is a potential objection, gather data on the projected return on investment (ROI), cost savings, and efficiency gains that justify the initial expenditure. Use case studies of other organizations that have successfully implemented similar solutions to demonstrate the feasibility and benefits.

Step 3: Address Objections in Your Presentation

Incorporate your responses to potential objections directly into your presentation. By addressing these concerns proactively, you show that you have thoroughly considered all aspects of your proposal and are prepared to handle any challenges that may arise.

For example, during your presentation, you might say, *"I understand that the initial cost is a significant consideration. However, let me share some data on the ROI and long-term savings that this investment will bring. Additionally, here are examples of how similar implementations have successfully benefited other organizations."*

Step 4: Use a Balanced Approach

When addressing objections, use a balanced approach that acknowledges the validity of the concerns while providing clear, evidence-based responses. Avoid dismissing objections outright, as this can come across as defensive or unempathetic.

For example, you might say, *"I understand that there are concerns about potential disruptions to our current workflows. While there will be an initial adjustment period, we have a detailed implementation plan that includes comprehensive training and support to ensure a smooth transition. The long-term benefits of improved efficiency and productivity will outweigh the temporary challenges."*

Step 5: Invite Questions and Dialogue

Encourage your audience to ask questions and express their concerns during or after your presentation. This open dialogue allows you to address any objections that you may not have anticipated and demonstrates your willingness to engage with your audience's perspectives.

For example, you could say, *"I invite you to share any concerns or questions you may have about this proposal. Your feedback is valuable, and I am here to address any issues to ensure we move forward with confidence."*

Step 6: Follow Up on Unresolved Concerns

If there are any objections or concerns that you are unable to fully address during the presentation, commit to following up with additional information or solutions. This proactive approach shows that you take their concerns seriously and are dedicated to finding resolutions.

For example, you might say, *"I understand that there are still some concerns about the timeline for implementation. I will gather more detailed information and follow up with you by the end of the week to provide a comprehensive plan."*

By addressing objections proactively, you can build trust and credibility with your audience, making your proposal more persuasive and increasing the likelihood of gaining their support.

Mastering the art of persuasion and influence is essential for effective leadership and business success. These skills not only help you achieve your goals but also foster a positive and collaborative work environment. Embrace these strategies to become a more influential and trusted leader.

By cultivating key leadership traits, inspiring and motivating your team, and mastering persuasion and influence, you can create an environment where everyone thrives. Remember, as Simon Sinek beautifully put it, true leadership is about caring for those in your charge, and empowering them to achieve greatness alongside you. With these principles, you'll lead with confidence and foster a culture of success and collaboration.

CHAPTER 7: LOOKING FORWARD – BUILDING A FUTURE WITH CONFIDENCE

"The best way to predict the future is to invent it."

– Alan Kay, American Computer Scientist

Alan Kay's words emphasize how much the future is within our control. The clock of business is always ticking, driven by the hands of new technology, changing societal values, and ever-evolving market demands. Start early and manage dynamically toward a forward-looking, innovative, and adaptable culture. Act today proactively to let a tomorrow be built, which not only can survive but can thrive when faced with aggressive challenges.

Facing the future in confidence means holistic steps that assure integration with work and life, which requires more than technological adoption; it means building a sustainable work-life integration system that takes care of our well-being and that of our teams. Balancing professional ambition with personal fulfillment is a must if we want to achieve success and related happiness in the long term. Leaders could advocate for flexibility in work arrangements, set clear boundaries, and promote wellness program implementations that support the team's overall well-being. This balance brings about a positive and motivated workforce ready for the challenges of tomorrow.

Staying Ahead with Technological Advancements

The rapid pace of technological innovation is transforming the way businesses operate. From artificial intelligence (AI) and machine learning to blockchain and the Internet of Things (IoT), emerging technologies are reshaping industries and creating new opportunities for growth and efficiency. Understanding the impact of these technologies on business is crucial for staying competitive in the modern market.

Emerging technologies can significantly enhance productivity by automating routine tasks, optimizing processes, and providing valuable insights through data analytics. For example, AI and machine learning can analyze large datasets to identify patterns and trends, enabling businesses to make more informed decisions. IoT devices can monitor and manage physical assets in real time, reducing downtime and improving operational efficiency. Blockchain technology offers enhanced security and transparency in transactions, which is particularly beneficial for industries such as finance and supply chain management.

In addition to operational benefits, these technologies can also transform customer experiences. AI-powered chatbots and virtual assistants provide personalized customer support, while augmented reality (AR) and virtual reality (VR) create immersive shopping experiences. By leveraging these technologies, businesses can better meet the evolving needs and expectations of their customers, fostering greater loyalty and satisfaction.

Strategies for Integrating New Technologies to Enhance Efficiency and Competitiveness

To effectively integrate new technologies and harness their potential, businesses must adopt a strategic approach. Here are some key strategies to consider:

1. Conduct Thorough Research and Assessment

Before implementing any new technology, it is essential to conduct thorough research to understand its capabilities, benefits, and potential challenges.

Here are some tips to consider:

- **Identify Business Needs:** Start by identifying the specific business needs that the new technology can address. Understand the pain points and areas where efficiency can be improved. This helps in selecting a technology that aligns well with your business objectives. For instance, if your business is facing issues with inventory management, you might look for technologies that offer advanced tracking and automation capabilities.
- **Evaluate Technology Capabilities:** Look into the capabilities of the technology in question. Understand how it works, what it offers, and its potential limitations. Compare it with other similar technologies to ensure you are choosing the best fit for your requirements. This might include reading reviews, consulting with current users, or attending demonstrations and webinars.
- **Assess Compatibility:** Check the compatibility of the new technology with your existing systems and infrastructure. Ensure that it can be integrated smoothly without causing disruptions to current operations. Compatibility issues can lead to significant downtime and additional costs, so it's crucial to identify these early on.
- **Cost-Benefit Analysis:** Perform a cost-benefit analysis to weigh the potential benefits against the costs involved. Consider not only the initial investment but also the long-term costs such as maintenance, training, and upgrades. For example, new software might be expensive initially but could lead to significant cost savings in the long run through increased efficiency.

- **Seek Expert Advice:** Consult with industry experts or technology consultants to gain insights and recommendations. Their expertise can provide valuable guidance and help you make informed decisions. This can also involve hiring external consultants who specialize in technology integration and can provide an unbiased perspective.

By thoroughly researching and assessing new technologies, you lay a strong foundation for successful integration, ensuring that the chosen technology meets your business needs and adds significant value.

2. Develop a Clear Implementation Plan

A well-defined implementation plan is crucial for the successful integration of new technologies.

Here are some steps to consider:

1. **Set Clear Objectives:** Define clear and achievable objectives for the implementation. Understand what success looks like and establish measurable goals to track progress. This might include specific targets such as improving production efficiency by 20% or reducing order processing time by half.
2. **Create a Timeline:** Develop a detailed timeline for the implementation process. Outline key milestones, deadlines, and deliverables to ensure the project stays on track. A Gantt chart can be a useful tool for visualizing the timeline and ensuring that all tasks are completed on schedule.
3. **Assign Responsibilities:** Clearly define roles and responsibilities for each team member involved in the implementation. Ensure that everyone knows their tasks and accountability. This can involve creating a responsibility assignment matrix (RAM) to clarify who is responsible for what.
4. **Communicate Effectively:** Establish a communication plan to keep all stakeholders informed and engaged. Regular updates and transparent communication help manage expectations and address any concerns promptly. Use regular meetings, emails, and project management tools to keep everyone aligned.
5. **Pilot Testing:** Conduct pilot tests to identify any potential issues before a full-scale rollout. This allows for adjustments and improvements based on real-world feedback. Pilot testing can help identify unexpected problems and provide an opportunity to train staff on a smaller scale.

A clear implementation plan provides a roadmap for seamless technology integration, helping to manage resources efficiently and achieve desired outcomes with minimal disruption.

3. Provide Comprehensive Training and Support
Effective training and support are essential to ensure that employees can use new technologies efficiently.

Here are some ways to ensure effective training:

- **Assess Training Needs:** Identify the specific skills and knowledge gaps that need to be addressed. This can be done through surveys, interviews, or assessments. Understanding the current skill levels of your employees will help tailor the training to meet their needs.
- **Develop Customized Training Programs:** Create training programs that are specifically designed to address the identified needs. These programs should be relevant, practical, and aligned with the daily tasks of the employees. Consider incorporating various formats such as workshops, e-learning modules, and hands-on sessions.
- **Utilize Experienced Trainers:** Hire experienced trainers who are well-versed in the new technology. They can provide in-depth knowledge and hands-on experience, ensuring that employees feel confident in using the technology. External trainers can also bring fresh perspectives and best practices from other implementations.
- **Incorporate Interactive Learning:** Use interactive learning methods such as simulations, role-playing, and gamification to make the training engaging and effective. Interactive training helps employees retain information better and apply what they have learned in real-world scenarios.
- **Provide Continuous Learning Opportunities:** Offer ongoing training and support to keep employees updated with the latest features and best practices. This can include refresher courses, advanced training sessions, and access to online resources. Encourage a culture of continuous learning where employees feel supported in their professional development.
- **Evaluate Training Effectiveness:** Assess the effectiveness of the training programs through feedback, assessments, and performance metrics. Use this information to make necessary adjustments and improvements. Regular evaluations ensure that the training remains relevant and effective.

By providing comprehensive training and support, businesses can empower their employees to fully utilize new technologies, enhancing productivity and ensuring a smoother transition.

4. Align Technology with Business Goals
Ensuring that new technology aligns with your overall business goals is crucial for maximizing its impact and value.

Here are some steps to consider:

1. **Strategic Alignment:** Before adopting any new technology, ensure it aligns with your organization's strategic goals and objectives. This involves understanding how the technology can support and enhance your business strategy. For example, if your goal is to improve customer service, look for technologies that streamline customer interactions and provide better insights into customer behavior.
2. **Stakeholder Involvement:** Engage key stakeholders from different departments in the decision-making process to ensure the technology meets the needs of the entire organization. This collaborative approach helps identify potential synergies and ensures broad support for the technology implementation. Involve stakeholders in discussions, pilot programs, and feedback sessions.
3. **Business Case Development:** Develop a robust business case that outlines the benefits of the new technology, including how it supports your business goals. This should include cost-benefit analysis, potential return on investment (ROI), and a clear plan for implementation. A well-developed business case helps secure buy-in from leadership and stakeholders.
4. **Integration with Existing Systems:** Plan for the seamless integration of new technology with your existing systems and processes. This involves assessing compatibility, potential disruptions, and required adjustments. Ensure that the technology can be integrated without causing significant operational issues or requiring extensive modifications to your existing infrastructure.
5. **Future-Proofing:** Consider the long-term implications of adopting new technology, including scalability, flexibility, and potential for future upgrades. Choose technologies that can grow with your business and adapt to changing needs. This forward-thinking approach helps avoid obsolescence and ensures sustained value.

Aligning new technologies with business goals ensures that your investments are strategically focused, driving meaningful improvements in efficiency, competitiveness, and overall business performance.

By understanding the impact of emerging technologies and adopting strategic approaches to their integration, businesses can enhance their efficiency, competitiveness, and ability to innovate. Staying ahead with technological advancements is not just about keeping up with trends but about leveraging these innovations to create sustainable growth and success in the future.

Cultivating Sustainable Work-Life Integration

In today's fast-paced and highly connected world, the lines between work and personal life often blur, leading to stress and burnout. Cultivating sustainable work-life integration is essential for maintaining overall well-being, productivity, and long-term career satisfaction. Unlike work-life balance, which implies a strict separation between work and personal life, work-life integration promotes a more harmonious blending of professional and personal responsibilities.

Strategies for Cultivating Sustainable Work-Life Integration

The following are some effective strategies to help individuals and organizations cultivate sustainable work-life integration:

1. Promote Flexible Work Arrangements

Flexible work arrangements refer to a variety of work schedules and environments that allow employees to manage their work responsibilities in ways that best suit their personal lives and work styles.

These arrangements can include options such:

- **Remote Work:** Employees work from a location outside the traditional office, such as their home or a co-working space. This arrangement reduces commuting time and can improve work-life balance.
- **Flexible Hours:** Employees have the flexibility to start and end their workday at times that differ from the standard office hours as long as they complete their required hours and meet their work commitments.
- **Compressed Workweek:** Employees work their total required hours over fewer days, such as four 10-hour days instead of five 8-hour days. This provides an additional day off each week.
- **Job Sharing:** Two or more employees share the responsibilities of a single full-time position, each working part-time hours. This allows employees to have more time for personal commitments while maintaining their careers.
- **Part-Time Work:** Employees work fewer hours than a full-time schedule, allowing them to balance work with other responsibilities or interests.

Implementing flexible work arrangements can lead to higher job satisfaction, increased productivity, and better work-life balance for employees.

Implementing Flexible Work Arrangements

Implementing flexible work arrangements requires thoughtful planning and clear communication to ensure both employees and the organization benefit from the new approach.

Here are steps to effectively implement flexible work arrangements:

Step 1: Assess Organizational Readiness

Before implementing flexible work arrangements, assess whether your organization is ready for this change. Consider factors such as the nature of the work, technology infrastructure, and management readiness. Some roles may require physical presence, while others can be performed remotely without any issues.

For example, customer-facing roles or positions that require access to specific equipment may need to be on-site, while administrative tasks, software development, and creative work can often be done remotely. Assessing organizational readiness ensures that flexible work arrangements are implemented where they can be most effective and least disruptive.

Step 2: Develop a Clear Policy

Create a detailed policy outlining the types of flexible work arrangements available, eligibility criteria, and expectations.

This policy should address the following:

- Types of flexible work options offered (e.g., remote work, flexible hours, compressed workweek, job sharing, part-time work).
- Criteria for eligibility (e.g., job roles, performance history).
- Guidelines for communication and availability (e.g., core hours, response time).
- Procedures for requesting and approving flexible work arrangements.
- Technology and security protocols for remote work.

Ensure the policy is transparent and accessible to all employees. For example, a clear policy might state that employees in roles that do not require physical presence on-site are eligible for remote work after six months of employment, provided they have demonstrated consistent performance and reliability.

Step 3: Provide Necessary Technology and Tools

Equip employees with the necessary technology and tools to work effectively from any location. This includes providing laptops, access to secure networks, collaboration tools (e.g., Zoom, Microsoft Teams), and project management software (e.g., Trello, Asana).

For example, ensure remote employees have secure VPN access to the company's network, use encrypted communication tools, and have training on cybersecurity best practices. Providing the right tools helps maintain productivity and data security.

Step 4: Train Managers and Employees

Training is crucial for the successful implementation of flexible work arrangements.

Managers should be trained on how to manage remote and flexible teams effectively, focusing on:

- Setting clear expectations and goals.
- Communicating effectively across different time zones and work schedules.
- Monitoring performance based on outcomes rather than hours worked.
- Supporting team cohesion and morale remotely.

Employees should be trained on best practices for working remotely, including time management, setting up a productive workspace, and maintaining clear communication with colleagues and supervisors.

Step 5: Pilot and Evaluate

Before fully rolling out flexible work arrangements, consider running a pilot program. This allows the organization to test the new arrangements, gather feedback, and make necessary adjustments.

For example, a three-month pilot program could involve a select group of employees working remotely or on flexible schedules. During this period, collect data on productivity, employee satisfaction, and any operational challenges.

After the pilot:

1. Evaluate the results.
2. Gather feedback from participants.
3. Refine the policy and procedures based on these insights.

This iterative approach helps identify potential issues and ensures a smoother implementation.

Step 6: Foster a Supportive Culture

Creating a culture that supports flexible work arrangements is essential for their success. Encourage open communication, trust, and accountability. Recognize and reward outcomes and achievements rather than focusing on hours worked.

For example, highlight success stories of employees who have effectively utilized flexible work arrangements to achieve high performance. Celebrate milestones and successes in team meetings, regardless of where employees are working from.

Step 7: Monitor and Adjust

Continuous monitoring and adjustment are vital to ensure the ongoing success of flexible work arrangements. Regularly review performance metrics, employee satisfaction surveys, and feedback to identify areas for improvement.

For instance, hold quarterly reviews to assess the impact of flexible work arrangements on productivity and morale. Be open to making adjustments, such as updating technology tools, revising policies, or providing additional training based on the feedback received.

By following these steps, organizations can implement flexible work arrangements that enhance employee satisfaction, boost productivity, and create a more adaptive and resilient workforce.

2. Set Boundaries

You need to set clear boundaries between work and personal life to maintain a healthy work-life integration. Boundaries help prevent burnout, reduce stress, and ensure that you can dedicate quality time to both your professional and personal responsibilities.

Here is how you can do this:

Step 1: Define Your Work Hours

Establishing clear work hours is fundamental to setting boundaries. Determine a schedule that works for you and your job requirements, and stick to it consistently. This means designating specific times for starting and ending your workday, as well as scheduling regular breaks. Clearly communicate these hours to your team and supervisors to set expectations about your availability.

For instance, if you decide that your workday will run from 9 AM to 5 PM, ensure that you log off and stop checking work emails after 5 PM. Use tools like calendar apps to block off your work hours and break times, and set reminders to help you adhere to this schedule. This consistency helps create a routine that delineates when you are in work mode and when you are in personal mode.

Step 2: Create a Dedicated Workspace

Having a dedicated workspace is crucial for maintaining a boundary between work and personal life. Choose a specific area in your home that is used exclusively for work. This could be a separate room, a corner of a room, or even a specific desk. The key is to associate this space with work activities only.

By creating a distinct workspace, you can mentally switch between work and relaxation. When you are in your designated workspace, you are in work mode, and when you leave that space, you leave work behind. This physical boundary helps reduce the temptation to work during personal time and vice versa. Ensure your workspace is comfortable, well-organized, and free from distractions to enhance productivity and focus.

Step 3: Set Digital Boundaries

Digital boundaries are essential in today's always-connected world. Establish rules for when and how you will use digital devices for work. This includes setting specific times for checking emails and turning off work-related notifications outside of work hours.

For example, you might decide to check emails only during designated times in the morning and afternoon rather than constantly throughout the day. Turn off notifications for work-related apps after your work hours to avoid being drawn back into work during your personal time. Use tools like "Do Not Disturb" modes on your devices to help enforce these boundaries.

Step 4: Communicate Boundaries with Others

Effective communication is key to maintaining boundaries. Inform your colleagues, supervisors, and clients about your work hours and availability. Make it clear when you will be reachable and when you will not, and encourage them to respect these boundaries.

For instance, you might include your work hours in your email signature or set an automatic reply during off-hours indicating when you will be available to respond. If someone contacts you outside of your designated work hours, respond during your next scheduled work period. By consistently communicating and enforcing your boundaries, you set the expectation that your personal time is to be respected.

Step 5: Prioritize and Delegate Tasks

To maintain boundaries, it's important to prioritize tasks and delegate when necessary. Focus on high-priority tasks during your designated work hours and be realistic about what you can accomplish within that time frame. Delegate tasks that can be handled by others to avoid overloading yourself.

Create a daily or weekly task list, ranking tasks by importance and deadline. Use productivity tools to keep track of your tasks and progress. If you find that your workload is consistently exceeding your work hours, have a discussion with your supervisor about redistributing tasks or extending deadlines. This proactive approach helps manage your workload effectively while preserving your personal time.

Step 6: Practice Self-Care

Incorporating self-care into your daily routine is essential for maintaining healthy boundaries. Dedicate time each day to activities that help you relax and recharge, such as exercise, hobbies, or spending time with loved ones. Self-care is not a luxury but a necessity for preventing burnout and maintaining overall well-being.

Schedule self-care activities just as you would schedule work tasks. Treat these activities as non-negotiable appointments with yourself. Whether it's a daily walk, reading a book, or practicing mindfulness, make sure these activities are a regular part of your routine. By prioritizing self-care, you reinforce the importance of your personal time and well-being.

Step 7: Reflect and Adjust

Regularly reflect on your boundaries and make adjustments as needed. Life circumstances and work demands can change, so it's important to revisit your boundaries periodically to ensure they are still effective and realistic.

Take time to assess how well your boundaries are working and identify any areas where you might need to make changes. For example, if you notice that you're frequently working late or feeling stressed, it might be time to adjust your work hours or set stricter digital boundaries. Continuously improving your boundary-setting practices helps maintain a sustainable work-life integration.

By following these steps, you can create clear boundaries that protect your personal time, reduce stress, and enhance both your work and personal life. Establishing and maintaining these boundaries is essential for long-term well-being and productivity.

3. Encourage Regular Breaks and Vacations

Encouraging regular breaks and vacations is a key strategy in promoting sustainable work-life integration. Taking regular breaks throughout the workday and ensuring employees use their vacation time is crucial for maintaining mental and physical health. Breaks allow employees to rest and recharge, which can lead to improved focus, reduced stress, and better overall job performance.

For example, studies have shown that taking short breaks throughout the day can improve concentration and reduce fatigue. Similarly, vacations can provide a much-needed reset, helping employees return to work refreshed and more productive.

Here's how to effectively implement this strategy:

Step 1: Set Clear Policies and Expectations

Establish clear policies that encourage employees to take regular breaks and use their vacation time.

These policies can include:

- **Scheduled Breaks:** Encourage employees to take short breaks throughout the day. For example, a 10-minute break every two hours can help maintain productivity and reduce stress.

- **Paid Time Off (PTO) Policies:** Ensure your PTO policies are generous and clearly communicated. Encourage employees to use their vacation days without feeling guilty or worried about job security.
- **Mandatory Vacations:** Some organizations implement mandatory vacation policies, where employees are required to take a minimum number of vacation days each year. This can help prevent burnout and ensure everyone gets the rest they need.

You need to clearly communicate these policies to all employees through the employee handbook, onboarding process, and regular reminders in team meetings and internal communications. Make it clear that taking breaks and vacations is not only allowed but encouraged and supported by the organization.

Step 2: Lead by Example

Managers and leaders should model the behavior they want to see in their teams. If leaders regularly take breaks and vacations, employees will feel more comfortable doing the same.

For instance, a manager can openly share their plans for taking a vacation and delegate their responsibilities during their absence. This not only shows that taking time off is acceptable but also demonstrates trust in the team's ability to manage in their absence.

Step 3: Promote a Culture of Health and Well-being

Create a work environment that prioritizes health and well-being. Encourage activities that promote relaxation and stress relief.

For example:

- Implement wellness programs that include yoga, meditation sessions, or fitness challenges.
- Provide resources such as mental health support, counseling services, or stress management workshops.
- Design office spaces with areas where employees can relax, such as quiet rooms, lounges, or outdoor spaces.

Step 4: Use Technology to Support Breaks and Vacations

Leverage technology to remind employees to take breaks and track their vacation time. There are various tools and apps designed to prompt employees to step away from their desks and to help manage PTO.

For example:

- Use software that alerts employees to take short breaks throughout the day.
- Implement a system that tracks PTO usage and sends reminders to employees who haven't used their vacation days.

Step 5: Monitor and Support

Regularly check in with employees to ensure they are taking breaks and using their vacation time. This can be part of regular performance reviews or one-on-one meetings.

For example, during a quarterly review, a manager might ask, "Have you been able to take regular breaks during your workday? When is your next planned vacation?" This approach shows that the organization values work-life balance and is committed to supporting it.

Step 6: Provide Adequate Coverage

Ensure that there are systems in place to cover work when employees are on vacation. This can include cross-training team members, hiring temporary staff, or redistributing tasks.

For example, create a coverage plan that outlines how responsibilities will be managed in an employee's absence. This might involve assigning key tasks to other team members or setting up an automated email response to manage expectations during the employee's time off.

Encouraging regular breaks and vacations is not just about preventing burnout; it is also about fostering a work environment where employees feel valued and supported. When employees know they can take time off to recharge without negative repercussions, they are more likely to be engaged, productive, and committed to their work.

Embracing the future with confidence means continually seeking ways to innovate, balance work and life, and leverage emerging technologies to stay ahead in the competitive business landscape. By fostering a culture of adaptability, promoting flexible work arrangements, and prioritizing employee well-being, you can build a resilient and forward-thinking organization. These strategies not only enhance efficiency and competitiveness but also create a supportive environment where both you and your team can thrive. As you move forward, remember that the journey of growth and improvement is ongoing. Stay committed to cultivating these practices, and you'll build a future that's not only successful but also fulfilling for everyone involved.

CONCLUSION

As this journey comes to a close, it is important to remember how empowering and confidence building it is within the business landscape. The lessons and strategies learned throughout the text of this book have been designed to create a strong foundation upon which up-and-coming entrepreneurs and business professionals can build a framework that will allow them to be successful in an ever-evolving and competitive environment. Now, empowerment and confidence are not just two words floating in the sea of the English language, but rather they constitute the very foundation upon which successful and satisfied careers are based.

Empowerment is taking charge of your journey and is having faith and confidence in the things you can achieve, making bold decisions towards your destiny with firmness and effectiveness. You are not a mere participant in your career; you are the architect behind its success. And that mindset shift enables you to tackle everything that comes your way with resilience, turning bumps in the road into opportunities for growth and innovation.

Confidence is the inner voice that fires your journey. It steadies your mind in the face of doubt; it gives you the boldness to voice your unique ideas—so important in building your confidence—and fortifies your belief that you are able to learn, grow, and be flexible. Confidence allows you to set high standards for yourself, be resilient, and remain focused in the face of setbacks. Empowerment and confidence together create a powerful synergy that will drive you forward and impact others through authentic leadership.

This book has examined ways to empower and build confidence in different areas, such as defining empowerment and confidence, building a foundation, and developing a capable and worthy mindset along with effective communication skills. It has also looked at the integral parts and purposes of networking, relationships, and inspirational leadership. The chapters provided strategies, examples, and real-life situations with practical steps to help you accomplish these skills.

This is no easy road toward empowerment and confidence. It involves introspection, continuous learning, and a preparedness to take risks. The world of business also includes uncertainties, market dynamics, and consistent pressures of proof. Being within those waves of doubt and uncertainty is where your true potential is built. Utilize principles of empowerment and confidence as you meet these challenges head-on and keep coming back, more giant than ever before, reborn like a phoenix to conquer another day.

In your entrepreneurial journey, remember that empowerment and confidence are not permanent conditions but akin to a moving target that changes placement over the course of time and reflection. They are the result of strong execution with the will to grow and take risks, fearlessly pursuing a bold goal. By living these principles, you not only achieve your success but also make a difference in your organization that ripples out to others.

This book is more than a roadmap toward business success; it is a call to live life with purpose, confidence, and fulfillment. It guides you to unleash your strengths, embrace your different path, and make meaningful strides toward your aspirations. The stories, insights, and exercises give you the material for inspiration to look deeply inside, for the opportunity to become audacious about a goal and then follow through with relentless pursuit.

In conclusion, the sentiment of empowerment and confidence emanates from within, driven by the belief of having the power to determine your destiny. Be it a startup, a small business, or career development, these are always the potential tools that will enable you to unfold your wings. They are the driving forces behind innovation, resilience, and lasting success. As you tread further on the path to progress, take these lessons with you, because the future belongs to those who bring it to life. Embrace the challenges, celebrate the victories, and let your empowered and confident self lead the way to a brighter, more successful future.

CONCLUSION

As this journey comes to a close, it is important to remember how empowering and confidence-building it is within the business landscape. The lessons and strategies learned throughout the text of this book have been designed to create a strong foundation upon which up-and-coming entrepreneurs and business professionals can build a framework that will allow them to be successful in an ever-evolving and competitive environment. Now, empowerment and confidence are not just two words floating in the sea of the English language, but rather, they constitute the very foundation upon which successful and satisfied careers are based.

Empowerment is taking charge of your journey, having faith and confidence in the things you can achieve, and making bold decisions towards your destiny with firmness and effectiveness. You are not a mere participant in your career; you are the architect behind its success. And that mindset shift enables you to tackle everything that comes your way with resilience, turning bumps in the road into opportunities for growth and innovation.

Confidence is the inner voice that fires your journey. It steadies your mind in the face of doubt; it gives you the boldness to voice your unique ideas—so important in building your confidence—and fortifies your belief that you are able to learn, grow, and be flexible. Confidence allows you to set high standards for yourself, be resilient, and remain focused in the face of setbacks. Empowerment and confidence together create a powerful synergy that will drive you forward and impact others through authentic leadership.

This book has examined ways to empower and build confidence in different areas, such as defining empowerment and confidence, building a foundation, and developing a capable and worthy mindset along with effective communication skills. It has also looked at the integral parts and purposes of networking, relationships, and inspirational leadership. The chapters provided strategies, examples, and real-life situations with practical steps to help you accomplish these skills.

This is no easy road toward empowerment and confidence. It involves introspection, continuous learning, and a preparedness to take risks. The world of business also includes uncertainties, market dynamics, and consistent pressures of proof. Being within those waves of doubt and uncertainty is where your true potential is built. Utilize principles of empowerment and confidence as you meet these challenges head-on and keep coming back, more giant than ever before, reborn like a phoenix to conquer another day.

In your entrepreneurial journey, remember that empowerment and confidence are not permanent conditions but akin to a moving target that changes placement over the course of time and reflection. They are the result of strong execution with the will to grow and take risks, fearlessly pursuing a bold goal. By living these principles, you not only achieve your success but also make a difference in your organization that ripples out to others.

This book is more than a roadmap toward business success; it is a call to live life with purpose, confidence, and fulfillment. It guides you to unleash your strengths, embrace your different paths, and make meaningful strides toward your aspirations. The stories, insights, and exercises give you the material for inspiration to look deeply inside, for the opportunity to become audacious about a goal, and then follow through with relentless pursuit.

In conclusion, the sentiment of empowerment and confidence emanates from within, driven by the belief in having the power to determine your destiny. Be it a startup, a small business, or career development, these are always the potential tools that will enable you to unfold your wings. They are the driving forces behind innovation, resilience, and lasting success. As you tread the path to progress, take these lessons with you because the future belongs to those who bring it to life. Embrace the challenges, celebrate the victories, and let your empowered and confident self lead the way to a brighter, more successful future.